TYPING   Made Simple

The Made Simple series
has been created
primarily for self-education
but can equally well
be used as
an aid to group study.
However complex the subject,
the reader is taken
step by step,
clearly and methodically
through the course. Each volume
has been prepared by
experts,
using throughout the
Made Simple technique of teaching.
Consequently the gaining
of knowledge now becomes
an experience to be enj~~~d

Accounting
Acting and Stagecraft
Additional Mathematics
Advertising
Anthropology
Applied Economics
Applied Mathematics
Applied Mechanics
Art Appreciation
Art of Speaking
Art of Writing
Biology
Book-keeping
British Constitution
Calculus
Chemistry
Childcare
Commerce
Commercial Law
Company Administration
Computer Programming
Cookery
Cost and Management
  Accounting
Data Processing
Dressmaking
Economic History
Economic and Social
  Geography
Economics
Electricity
Electronic Computers

Electronics
English
French
Geology
German
Human Anatomy
Italian
Journalism
Latin
Law
Management
Marketing
Mathematics
Modern European History
New Mathematics
Office Practice
Organic Chemistry
Philosophy
Photography
Physical Geography
Physics
Pottery
Psychology
Rapid Reading
Russian
Salesmanship
Soft Furnishing
Spanish
Statistics
Transport and
  Distribution
Typing

TYPING   Made Simple

Nathan Levine

Advisory editor
Margaret Davis

Made Simple Books
W. H. ALLEN   London
A Howard & Wyndham Company

© 1957 by Doubleday & Company, Inc., and completely reset
and revised 1967 by W. H. Allen & Co. Ltd.

Made and printed in Great Britain
by Richard Clay (The Chaucer Press), Ltd., Bungay, Suffolk
for the publishers W. H. Allen & Co. Ltd.
44 Hill Street, London W1X 8LB

First edition April 1967
Reprinted January 1970
Second (revised) edition April 1971
Reprinted October 1972
Third (revised) edition November 1974
Reprinted December 1976

ISBN 0 491 01940 8 paperbound

Foreword

Today the typewriter is indispensable as a means of communication, both in business and in private life. This book has been planned especially for the beginner, using as simple an approach as is compatible with the achievement of a good standard. The exercises are so graduated that any student who attains a reasonable degree of accuracy in each of them before proceeding to the next will have no difficulty in becoming a proficient typist. Learning is systematic and progressive because each lesson allows for refreshing the student's memory of the previous lesson before introducing new topics.

Two charts of the typewriter keyboard are printed at the beginning of the book. One should be cut out and placed upright beside the typewriter during most of the course—until the keyboard is thoroughly memorized; the other copy can be kept as a spare.

Although *Typing Made Simple* is designed primarily for self-study, it can be used with advantage by the teacher in the classroom. It can also serve as an excellent introductory course for anyone working up to specific typing examinations, such as those set by the Royal Society of Arts. Indeed, with the method used in this book, beginners will be surprised at the speed and facility with which they will be able to master the skill of typewriting.

MARGARET DAVIS

v

Table of Contents

LESSON 12

LESSON 13

LESSON 14

LESSON 15

LESSON 20

LESSON 21

LESSON 22

LESSON 23

LESSON 24

1 Margins Left/Right
2 Carriage End Covers
3 Carriage Release
4 Paper Guide Scale
5 Paper Guide
6 Line Space Selector
7 Variable Spacer
8 Platen Knob
9 Paper Bail
10 Card Holder
11 Ribbon Reverse
12 Ribbon Release
13 Carriage Return Lever
14 Tab Clear Key
15 Back Space Key
16 Shift Lock
17 Left/Right Shift Key
18 Paper Table
19 Paper Bail Scale
20 Paper Release Lever
21 Ribbon Carrier
22 Ribbon Colour & Stencil Control
23 Ribbon Selector
24 Margin Release
25 Tab Set Key
26 Tabulator Bar
27 Space Bar

THE TYPEWRITER AND ITS PARTS
(Olivetti Typewriter)

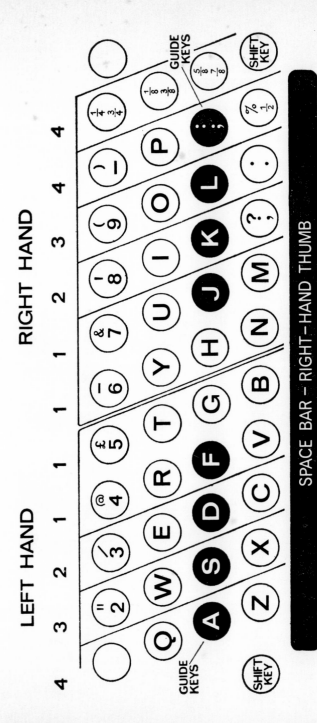

LEFT HAND   RIGHT HAND

GUIDE KEYS

SPACE BAR – RIGHT–HAND THUMB

The four keys on the left-hand side ASDF and the four keys on the right-hand side JKL; are the "home keys". These are the resting places over which the four fingers of the left and right hands must remain, except when it is necessary to remove a finger in order to strike a key. After striking the key the finger must be returned immediately to its correct position.

TYPING MADE SIMPLE

LESSON 1

Aim: To learn—
  (*a*) The **Home-Key** position.
  (*b*) To use the keys **F J R U.**

Step One—Preparing To Type

1. Centre the Carriage.
The carriage is the movable part of the typewriter that holds the cylinder.

  (*a*) Hold the right cylinder knob and with the same hand depress the carriage release—the spring near the knob. (See Fig. 1.)

Fig. 1. Centring the Carriage by Using the Carriage Release.

1

   (*b*) Move the carriage left or right and stop it at the centre of the typewriter.

   (*c*) Remove your hand from the carriage release.

2. Adjust the Paper Guide at 0.

The paper guide is a strip of metal at the left end of the carriage; it guides the paper into the machine.

Slide the paper guide until its vertical edge points to 0 on the paper guide scale. (See Fig. 2.)

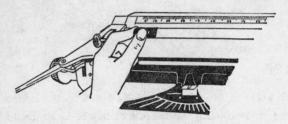

Fig. 2. Adjusting the Paper Guide at 0.

3. Insert the Paper.

   (*a*) Hold the paper with the thumb and four fingers of your left hand.

   (*b*) Place the paper squarely behind the cylinder, left edge against the paper guide.

   (*c*) Place your thumb under the right cylinder knob and the first two fingers on top.

   (*d*) Now give the knob a sudden spin. (See Fig. 3.)

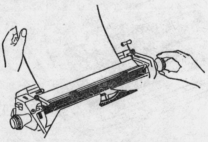

Fig. 3. Inserting the Paper.

4. Adjust the Paper Bail.

Place the paper bail over the paper and move the small rollers so that they are spaced equally across the paper. (See Fig. 4.)

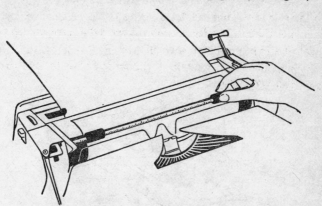

Fig. 4. Adjusting the Paper Bail and the Small Rollers.

5. Straighten the Paper.

Your paper is straight if the left edge of the front part is even with the left edge of the back part—and both edges even with the paper guide.

(*a*) If your paper is not straight, depress the paper release and straighten the paper.

(*b*) Now hold the paper in place with your left hand, and with the other push the paper release back to position. (See Fig. 5.)

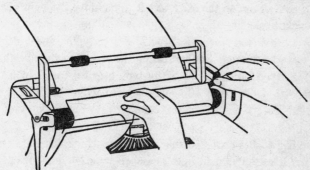

Fig. 5. Straightening the Paper.

NOTE: (*a*) Use the Paper Release to remove the paper from the machine.

(*b*) Return the Paper Release to position when paper is removed.

6. Set the Line Space Gauge for Single Spacing.

The Line Space Gauge is a lever above the left end of the cylinder; it regulates the spacing between lines—single, double, or triple.

Move the Line Space Gauge to '1' for single spacing. (See Fig. 6.)

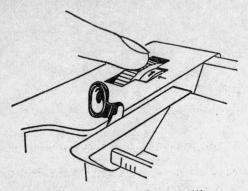

Fig. 6. Line Space Gauge at '1'.

7. Set the Margin Stops.

The margin stops set the points at which the typing line begins and ends.

(*a*) Clear the margin stops now set on your machine. First move the left one to the extreme left; then move the right one to the extreme right.

(*b*) With a ruler, measure 5 inches on the typing line scale. This is the numbered scale indicating the length of the line that may be typed and the number of typing spaces to the inch.

(*c*) If 5 inches cover 50 spaces, your machine has **Pica** type—10 spaces to the inch. In this case, set your margin stops at 15 and 70.

(*d*) If 5 inches cover 60 spaces, your machine has **Elite** type—12 spaces to the inch. In this case, set your margin stops at 25 and 80.

Follow this procedure:

1st: Move the carriage until the printing point indicator points to the left margin; then set the margin stop.

2nd: Move the carriage until the printing point indicator points to the right margin; then set the margin stop. (See Fig. 7.)

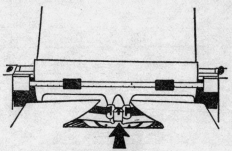

Fig. 7. Printing Point Indicator.

NOTE: The systems of margin stops on various machines are generally found in three variations:

(1) At the back of the paper rest, controlled by levers.
(2) At the back of the paper rest, controlled by hand.
(3) At the front, controlled by hand.

8. Leave a 1½-inch Top Margin.

You can type 6 lines to the inch from top to bottom.

(*a*) Turn the cylinder knob backward until the top edge of the paper is level with the alignment scale. (See Fig. 8.)

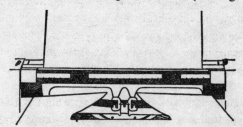

Fig. 8. Top Edge of Paper Level with Alignment Scale.

(*b*) Strike the line-space lever 10 times with your left hand.

By typing on the 10th line from the top edge of the paper you leave a top margin of 9 lines—1½ inches. (See Fig. 9.)

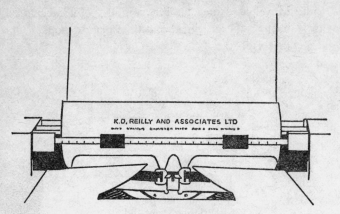

K.O. REILLY AND ASSOCIATES LTD

Fig. 9. 1½ Inch Top Margin (10 spaces from top edge).

Step Two—Learning To Type

1. Assume Correct Typing Posture.
    (*a*) Sit erect, both feet flat on the floor, body bent slightly forward.
    (*b*) Place left hand on A S D F (Little finger on A).
    (*c*) Place right hand on J K L ; (Little finger on;).
    (*d*) Curve all fingers like claws. Rest fingertips very lightly on centre of keys.
    (*e*) Slant hands upward from the wrists. Keep wrists low but not touching the machine.
    (*f*) Keep elbows close to your sides.
    (See Fig. 10.)

2. How to Strike the Keys.
    (*a*) Feel the F key with the left first finger.
    (*b*) Lift all four fingers slightly and strike the F key sharply with the fingertip.

Fig. 10. Fingers on Home Keys.

(*c*) Strike the F key again—HARD. Let your finger spring back—as though the key were red hot. Strike the F key a few more times.

(*d*) Practise half a line of f's as shown below.

fffffffffffffffffffffffffff

(*e*) Now using the right first finger, strike the J key—sharply. Release the key instantly—as though it were red hot. Try it a few more times. Practise half a line of j's. Now your line looks like this:

fffffffffffffffffffffffffffffffjjjjjjjjjjjjjjjjjjjjjjjjjjjj

3. How to Use the Space Bar.

Spaces are made by striking the space bar, at the bottom of the keyboard, with the side of the right thumb—sharply. The left thumb does no work; so curve it slightly under the first finger.

(*a*) Try out the space bar by striking it quickly and sharply with the side of the right thumb.

(*b*) Type the following line of fff jjj, spacing between each group of letters:

fff jjj fff jjj fff jjj fff jjj fff jjj fff jjj

4. How to 'Throw' the Carriage.

After each typewritten line, the carriage must be returned to the starting point. Returning the carriage is called 'throwing' the carriage. This is done by means of the line-space lever. (See Fig. 11.)

Fig. 11. 'Throwing' the Carriage.

(*a*) Hold the fingers of your left hand close together, palm down.

(*b*) Bring the tip of the first finger to the line-space lever. Keep your right hand on the home keys.

(*c*) Strike the line-space lever and quickly return the hand to the home keys.

5. Self-Testing Work: Now test yourself. See how well you can strike F and J keys and the space bar. See how quickly you can 'throw' the carriage and return your left hand to home position. Type the following three lines exactly as shown:

TYPING TIP: *Throw the carriage with a flip of the wrist.*

```
fff jjj fff jjj fff jjj fff jjj fff jjj fff jjj
fff jjj fff jjj fff jjj fff jjj fff jjj fff jjj
fff jjj fff jjj fff jjj fff jjj fff jjj fff jjj
```

Now stop typing and **relax.**

6. Learning to use New Keys: R U.

R is controlled by the F finger.

U is controlled by the J finger.

Step 1—New Key Preview

(Feeling the Keys—to Memorize the Reach)

R: Look at the keyboard. To reach R, move the F finger up and slightly to the left. Feel the centre of the R key—with the fingertip. Return the finger quickly to the F key. Reach for R and return to F—several times. Try it without looking at the keyboard. Look at the chart.

U: To reach U, move the J finger up and slightly to the left. Feel the centre of the U key—with the fingertip. Return the finger quickly to the J key. Reach for U and return to J—several times. Try it without looking at the keyboard. Look at the chart.

Step 2—New Key Try-out

Strike Keys Sharply.

```
r r r r frf frf frf frf u u u u juj juj juj juj
frf juj frf juj frf juj frf juj frf juj frf juj
```

Now stop typing and **relax.**

7. **Self-Testing Work:** You have learned the location of **F J R U.** Now test yourself. See how confidently you can strike these keys without looking at your fingers. Look at the chart. Type the following 6 lines exactly as shown:

TYPING TIP: *Think of the finger and the key it controls.*

Throw the carriage twice after every second line.

```
fff jjj fff jjj fff jjj fff jjj fff jjj fff jjj
fff jjj fff jjj fff jjj fff jjj fff jjj fff jjj

fru fru fru jur jur jur ruj ruj ruj urf urf urf
fur fur fur ruf ruf ruf urj urj urj fuj fuj fuj

urf urf urf juf juf juf fuj fuj fuj fru fru fru
fur fur fur ruf ruf ruf urf urf urf jur jur jur
```

Now take a moment to relax.

8. **Improvement Work:** Type another copy of the above 6 lines. See if you can type them more smoothly and more accurately.

LESSON 2

Aim: To learn to use **D K E I**.

1. Machine Adjustments:
   (*a*) Paper Guide: At 0.
   (*b*) Line Space Gauge: For single spacing.
   (*c*) Margin Stops: For **Pica** type........................at 15 and 70.
   For **Elite** type ....at 25 and 80.
   (*d*) Top Margin: 1½ inches. (Type on 10th line from top edge.)

2. Warm-up: (5 Minutes) Type the following 4 lines exactly as shown. If you finish ahead of time, type them again.

REMINDER: Strike the space bar with the side of your right thumb.
Throw the carriage twice after the second line.

```
fff jjj fff jjj fff jjj fff jjj fff jjj fff jjj
frf juj frf juj frf juj frf juj frf juj frf juj

fur fur fur ruf ruf ruf jur jur jur ruj ruj ruj
urj urj urj juf juf juf fuj fuj fuj fur fur fur
```

3. New Key Control: (10 Minutes)
   (*a*) Learning to use New Keys: **D K**.
   D is controlled by the second finger of your left hand.
   K is controlled by the second finger of your right hand.

Step 1—New Key Preview

(Feeling the Keys—to Memorize the Reach)

Feel the centre of the **D** and **K** keys. As you feel each key, think of the finger and the key it controls.

To type **D** and **K**, raise all four fingers slightly from the wrist and strike the key sharply with the fingertip. Strike the key as though it were red hot. Keep all fingers curved like claws—close to home keys.

10

Step 2—New Key Try-out

```
d d d d ddd ddd ddd ddd k k k k kkk kkk kkk kkk
ddd kkk ddd kkk ddd kkk ddd kkk ddd kkk ddd kkk
```

(*b*) Learning to use **New Keys: E I.**
     E is controlled by the **D** finger.
     I is controlled by the **K** finger.

Step 1—New Key Preview

(Feeling the Keys—to Memorize the Reach)

E: To reach **E**, move the **D** finger up and slightly to the left. Feel the centre of the **E** key—with the fingertip. Return the finger quickly to the **D** key. Reach for **E** and return to **D**—several times. Try it without looking at the keyboard. Look at the chart.

I: To reach **I**, move the **K** finger up and slightly to the left. Feel the centre of the **I** key—with the fingertip. Return the finger quickly to the **K** key. Reach for **I** and return to **K**—several times. Try it without looking at the keyboard. Look at the chart.

Step 2—New Key Try-out

```
e e e e ded ded ded ded ded i i i i kik kik kik
ded kik ded kik ded kik ded kik ded kik ded kik
```

4. Self-Testing Work: (25 Minutes) Test your mastery of the new keys in this lesson. Type the following 12 lines exactly as shown. Don't rush. Think of the finger and the key it controls.

TYPING TIP: *Throw the carriage with a flip of the wrist.*
         Keep right hand on home keys.

```
did did did ire ire ire rid rid rid eke eke eke
rid rid rid eke eke eke ire ire ire did did did

kid kid kid fee fee fee red red red fir fir fir
red red red fir fir fir fee fee fee kid kid kid

free free free juke juke juke fire fire fire juke
fire fire fire juke juke juke free free free juke
```

```
deer deer deer rude rude rude dire dire dire ride
rude rude rude dire dire dire deer deer deer ride

fired fired fired rider rider rider freed freed
rider rider rider freed freed freed fired fired

did red ire fee rid deer rude fire feed juke rider
rid fee ire red did juke fire rude juke deed freed
```

5. Corrective Work: (10 Minutes)

(*a*) Compare your work carefully with the above 12 lines.

(*b*) Draw a line under each word in which you find an error. Write a list of these words on a separate sheet of paper.

(*c*) Practise each word 3 times as shown in the following sample:

```
freed freed freed rider rider rider fired fired fired
```

NOTE: (*a*) A warning bell rings when the carriage is about 7 spaces from the right margin.

(*b*) When you hear the bell, finish the word you are typing and throw the carriage for a new line.

(*d*) When you finish the **Corrective Work,** stop typing and **relax.**

6. Improvement Work: (25 Minutes) Try another copy of the same 12 lines. See if you can type them more smoothly and more accurately.

LESSON 3

Aim. To learn to use the keys **T Y G H**.

1: Machine Adjustments: See Lesson 2.

2. Warm-up: (5 Minutes) Copy the following 6 lines exactly as shown. If you finish ahead of time, type another copy.

TYPING TIP: *Strike keys sharply. Return fingers quickly to home keys.*

```
fff jjj ddd kkk frf juj ded kik fff jjj ddd kkk
frf juj ded kik fur fur kid kid red red ire ire

kid kid kid juke juke juke dire dire dire fire
rid rid rid rude rude rude ride ride ride feed

did red ire fee rid deer rude fire feed juke rider
rid fee ire red did juke fire rude juke deed freed
```

3. New Key Control: (10 Minutes)

    (*a*) Learning to use New Keys: **T Y**.

        T is controlled by the **F** finger.

        Y is controlled by the **J** finger.

Step 1—New Key Preview

Feel the centre of each new key—and memorize its location. Do not look at your fingers. Look at the chart. Think of the finger and the key it controls.

Step 2—New Key Try-out

        Strike key sharply. Return finger to home base.

```
t t t t ftf ftf ftf ftf y y y y jyj jyj jyj jyj
ftf jyj ftf jyj ftf jyj ftf jyj ftf jyj ftf jyj
```

    (*b*) Learning to use New Keys: **G H**.

        G is controlled by the **F** finger.

        H is controlled by the **J** finger.

13

Step 1—New Key Preview

Reach and feel each new key several times. Return the finger quickly to home base. Memorize the new key location. Think of the finger and the key it controls. Use the chart as a guide.

Step 2—New Key Try-out

Strike sharply. Return quickly.

```
g g g g fgf fgf fgf fgf h h h h jhj jhj jhj jhj
fgf jhj fgf jhj fgf jhj fgf jhj fgf jhj fgf jhj
```

(c) Word Drill. Containing New Keys: **T Y G H**.

```
hit hit hit hit hit hit get get get get get get
yet yet yet yet yet yet try try try try try try
```

4. **Self-Testing Work:** (25 Minutes) Test your mastery of the new keys in this lesson. Copy the following 14 lines exactly as shown:

Throw carriage twice after every second line.

```
the the the try try try get get get yet yet yet
try try try the the the yet yet yet get get get

key key key hit hit hit tie tie tie kit kit kit
tie tie tie kit kit kit key key key hit hit hit

here here here they they they true true true
they they they true true true here here here

there there there fruit fruit fruit right right right
fruit fruit fruit right right right there there there

third third third tired tired tired urged urged urged
tired tired tired urged urged urged third third third

truth truth truth their their their dried dried dried
their their their dried dried dried truth truth truth

did they get the right dried fruit there yet
did they get the right dried fruit there yet
```

5. **Corrective Work:** (10 Minutes) Make a list of the words in which you find errors; then practise each word 3 times. REMINDER: When you hear the bell, finish the word you are typing and throw carriage for next line.

6. **Improvement Work:** (25 Minutes) Type another copy of the above 14 lines. Try to turn out a better piece of work

LESSON 4

Aim: To learn to use the keys **S L W O.**

1. Machine Adjustments: See Lesson 2.

2. Warm-up: (5 Minutes) Copy the first two lines exactly as shown; then throw the carriage twice and type the sentence 10 times.

```
frf juj ded kik ftf jyj fgf jhj frf juj ded kik
ded kik ftf jyj fgf jhj frf juj ded kik ftf jyj

they urged her to get the right dried fruit there
```

3. New Key Control: (10 Minutes)
    (*a*) Learning to use New Keys: **S L.**
        S is controlled by the left third finger.
        L is controlled by the right third finger.

Step 1—New Key Preview

Feel the centre of each new key—with the fingertip. Think of the finger and the key it controls. Refer to the chart.

Step 2—New Key Try-out

Strike keys sharply. Let go instantly. Keep all fingers curved.

```
s s s s sss sss sss sss l l l l lll lll lll lll
sss lll sss lll sss lll sss lll sss lll sss lll
```

    (*b*) Learning to use New Keys: **W O.**
        W is controlled by the **S** finger.
        O is controlled by the **L** finger.

16

Step 1—New Key Preview

Reach and feel each new key several times. Return finger quickly to home base. Memorize new-key location. Think of the finger and the key it controls.

Step 2—New Key Try-out

Strike keys sharply. Return fingers quickly to home base.

w w w w sws sws sws sws o o o o lol lol lol lol
sws lol sws lol sws lol sws lol sws lol sws lol

(c) Word Drill. Containing New Keys: **S L W O.**

Don't move your arms. Let your fingers do the work.

sow sow sow sow sow sow low low low low low low
row row row row row row how how how how how how

4. **Self-Testing Work:** (25 Minutes) Test yourself. See how well you have trained your fingers to locate the new keys in this lesson. Copy the following 20 lines exactly as shown:

Do not strike one letter over another.
Don't worry about errors.
Keep your eyes on this page.
Finish every line you start.

is is is so so so of of of do do do go go go to to to
go go go to to to do do do of of of so so so is is is

too too too low low low set set set wit wit wit wit
sit sit sit lit lit lit wit wit wit low low low low

wool wool wool suit suit suit full full full wood wood
hole hole hole wool wool wool suit suit suit good good

style style style order order order those those
loose loose loose style style style order order

desire desire desire rulers rulers rulers worker
worker worker worker desire desire desire rulers

hold your wrists low while you strike the keys
hold your wrists low while you strike the keys

```
we desire the right goods for our wool suits
we desire the right goods for our wool suits

if you will go with us you will see the fleet
if you will go with us you will see the fleet

we will try to fill your order for the wool suits
we will try to fill your order for the wool suits

if we get the right goods we will fill your order
if we get the right goods we will fill your order
```

5. **Corrective Work:** (10 Minutes) Check your work carefully. Make a list of the words in which you find errors; then practise each word 3 times.

6. **Improvement Work:** (25 Minutes) Type another copy of the above 20 lines. See if you can type them more smoothly and more accurately.

LESSON 5

Aim: To learn to use the keys **A ;** (Semicolon) **Q P.**

1. Machine Adjustments: See Lesson 2.

2. Warm-up: (5 Minutes) Copy the first two lines exactly as shown; then throw the carriage twice and type the sentence 10 times.

```
frf juj ded kik ftf jyj fgf jhj frf juj ftf jyj fgf jhj
ded kik sws lol ded kik sws lol frf juj ftf jyj fgf jhj

we will fill your order for the wool suits this week
```

3. New Key Control: (10 Minutes)
  (*a*) Learning to use New Keys: **A ;**
   A is controlled by the left little finger.
   ; is controlled by the right little finger.

Step 1—New Key Preview

Feel the centre of each new key—with the fingertip. Think of the finger and the key it controls—to memorize the new key location.

Step 2—New Key Try-out

Strike keys sharply. Keep elbows close to your sides.

```
a a a a aaa aaa aaa aaa ; ; ; ; ;;; ;;; ;;; ;;;
aaa ;;; aaa ;;; aaa ;;; aaa ;;; aaa ;;; aaa ;;;
```

  (*b*) Learning to use New Keys: **Q P.**
   Q is controlled by the **A** finger.
   P is controlled by the **;** finger.

19

Step 1—New Key Preview

Reach and feel each new key—several times. Return finger quickly to home base. Think of the finger and the key it controls—to memorize the reach.

Step 2—New Key Try-out

Strike keys hard.

```
q q q q aqa aqa aqa aqa p p p p ;p; ;p; ;p; ;p;
aqa ;p; aqa ;p; aqa ;p; aqa ;p; aqa ;p; aqa ;p;
```

(*c*) Word Drill. Containing New Keys: **A ; Q P.**

```
pa; pa; pa; pa; pa; pa; up; up; up; up; up; up;
pa; pa; pa; pa; pa; pa; up; up; up; up; up; up;
```

```
quay quay quay quay quay quip quip quip quip quip
quay quay quay quay quay quip quip quip quip quip
```

4. Self-Testing Work: (25 Minutes) Test your mastery of the new keys in this lesson. Copy the following 20 lines exactly as shown:

TYPING RULE: Space once after a semicolon.

REMINDER: Strike space bar with side of right thumb.

TYPING TIP: *Strike every key with equal force.*

```
apt apt apt; put put put; sip sip sip; hip hip hip;
sip sip sip; hip hip hip; apt apt apt; put put put;

quip quip quip; quit quit quit; aqua aqua aqua;
aqua aqua aqua; quip quip quip; quit quit quit;

paid paid paid; pair pair pair; pass pass pass;
pair pair pair; pass pass pass; paid paid paid;

quote quote quote; paper paper paper; quite quite;
paper paper paper; quite quite quite; quote quote;

prefer prefer prefer; prepay prepay prepay; quires;
prepay prepay prepay; prefer prefer prefer; quires;

postage postage postage; quarter quarter quarter;
poultry poultry poultry; quality quality quality;
```

```
two quires of high quality paper were shipped today;
two quires of high quality paper were shipped today;

we shall pay you well to prepare the reports for us;
we shall pay you well to prepare the reports for us;

we quote a low figure for our high quality paper;
we quote a low figure for our high quality paper;

we prefer to prepay the postage for the two quires;
we prefer to prepay the postage for the two quires;
```

5. Corrective Work: (10 Minutes) Check your work carefully. Make a list of the words in which you find errors. Practise each word 3 times.

6. Improvement Work: (25 Minutes) Try another copy of the above 20 lines—for better result. See if you can turn out a more accurate job.

LESSON 6

Aim: To learn to use the **Shift Keys** for **Capital Letters**.

1. Machine Adjustments: See Lesson 2.

2. Warm-up: (5 Minutes) Copy the first two lines exactly as shown; then throw the carriage twice and type the sentence 10 times. The sentence contains every letter you have learned thus far.

```
frf juj ftf jyj fgf jhj ded kik sws lol aqa ;p;
aqa ;p; sws lol ded kik frf juj ftf jyj fgf jhj

he will pay jed squire for the sugar this week;
```

3. New Key Control: (10 Minutes) Learning to use the **shift keys**.

To make a **Capital letter**, depress the **shift key** firmly with the little finger of the opposite hand and strike the letter to be **capitalized**. Be sure to hold the **shift key** down until you have struck the letter.

Step 1—Shift Key Try-out

(*a*) Depress the left **shift key**; then return the finger to **A**.

(*b*) Depress the **shift key**; then return the finger to semicolon.

(*c*) Practise the left and right **shift key** manipulation until you can perform it smoothly. (See Figs. 12, 13.)

Step 2—Capital Letter Drill

Hold down the shift key until you have struck the letter.
Return the little finger to its home key.

```
F F F F F F F Fa Fa Fa Fa Fa Fa Fay Fay Fay Fay Fay Fay
J J J J J J J Ja Ja Ja Ja Ja Ja Jay Jay Jay Jay Jay Jay

R R R R R R R Ra Ra Ra Ra Ra Ra Ray Ray Ray Ray Ray Ray
H H H H H H H Ha Ha Ha Ha Ha Ha Hal Hal Hal Hal Hal Hal
```

Fig. 12. Using Left Shift Key.　　**Fig. 13.** Using Right Shift Key.

4. Self-Testing Work: (25 Minutes) Test your mastery of the **shift key.**
Copy the following 22 lines exactly as shown:

REMINDER: Space once after a semicolon.

```
Kay Kay Kay; Joe Joe Joe; Alf Alf Alf; Lou Lou Lou;
Joe Joe Joe; Kay Kay Kay; Lou Lou Lou; Alf Alf Alf;

Dora Dora Dora; Ella Ella Ella; Pete Pete Pete;
Sara Sara Sara; Lola Lola Lola; Will Will Will;

Garry Garry Garry; Harry Harry Harry; Paula Paula;
Harry Harry Harry; Taffy Taffy Taffy; Quill Quill;

Uriah Uriah Uriah; Yetta Yetta Yetta; Ollie Ollie;
Yetta Yetta Yetta; Ollie Ollie Ollie; Uriah Uriah;

Walter Walter Walter; Esther Esther Esther; Isaiah;
Esther Esther Esther; Walter Walter Walter; Isaiah;

Arthur Arthur Arthur; Lester Lester Lester; Philip;
Qualey Qualey Qualey; Arthur Arthur Arthur; Philip;

Joseph likes to study; Joseph likes to study art;
Joseph likes to study; Joseph likes to study art;

Esther will write; Esther will write Larry today;
Esther will write; Esther will write Larry today;
```

```
Arthur likes; Arthur likes to play the flute;
Arthur likes; Arthur likes to play the flute;

Kate says; Kate says she will stay till Friday;
Kate says; Kate says she will stay till Friday;

Paul will take Willa to the Park Sherry Theatre;
Paul will take Willa to the Park Sherry Theatre;
```

5. **Corrective Work:** (10 Minutes) Make a list of the words in which you find errors; then practise each word 3 times.

6. **Improvement Work:** (25 Minutes) Type another copy of the above 22 lines—for better result.

LESSON 7

Aim: (*a*) To learn to use the **Shift Lock**.

(*b*) To learn to use the : (Colon).

1. Machine Adjustments: See Lesson 2.

2. Warm-up: (5 Minutes) Copy the first two lines exactly as shown; then throw the carriage twice and type the sentence 10 times—to give you practice on all the letters you have learned so far.

```
frf juj ftf jyj fgf jhj ded kik sws lol aqa ;p;
aqa ;p; sws lol ded kik frf juj ftf jyj fgf jhj
```

```
He will pay Jed Squire for the sugar this week;
```

3. New Key Control: (10 Minutes) Learning to use the **shift lock**. The **shift lock** is a time-saving device which enables you to type a series of **capital letters**.

Step 1—Shift Lock Try-out

(*a*) With your left little finger, depress the **shift lock**—then return the finger quickly to its home key. The machine is now **locked** for typing **capital letters**.

(*b*) Now with the same little finger, strike the **shift key**—then return the finger quickly to its home key. The machine is now unlocked—for regular typing.

(*c*) Repeat the above exercise several times until you develop the knack of **locking** and unlocking the machine.

Step 2—Shift Lock Drill

```
It is GOOD WORK; It is GOOD WORK; It is GOOD WORK;
It is GOOD WORK; It is GOOD WORK; It is GOOD WORK;
```

4. Self-Testing Work: (20 Minutes) Copy the following 15 lines exactly as shown. To make a colon (:), depress the left shift key and strike the semicolon (;) key.

Space twice after a colon.

```
frf juj ftf jyj fgf jhj ded kik sws lol aqa ;p;
The TITLE of the REPORT is: HOUSES FOR SALE
The TITLE of the REPORT is: HOUSES FOR SALE

aqa ;p; sws lol ded kik frf juj ftf jyj fgf jhj
We quote LOW FIGURES for HIGHEST QUALITY paper;
We quote LOW FIGURES for HIGHEST QUALITY paper;

frf juj ftf jyj fgf jhj ded kik sws lol aqa ;p;
The PARK POSTER reads: KEEP OFF THE GRASS
The PARK POSTER reads: KEEP OFF THE GRASS

aqa ;p; sws lol ded kik frf juj ftf jyj fgf jhj
Paul quoted the old adage: THE THRIFTY ARE WISE
Paul quoted the old adage: THE THRIFTY ARE WISE

frf juj ftf jyj fgf jhj ded kik sws lol aqa ;p;
You should STRIKE ALL THE KEYS with EQUAL POWER;
You should STRIKE ALL THE KEYS with EQUAL POWER;
```

5. Corrective Work: (10 Minutes) Make a list of the words in which you find errors; then practise each word 3 times.

6. Improvement Work: (20 Minutes) Type another copy of the above 15 lines to strengthen your control of the **shift lock** and the **shift key.**

7. Challenge Work: (10 Minutes) Here's a challenge to you: 9 new lines. Try for a **perfect** copy.

Keep your mind on your work. Think as you type.

```
frf juj ftf jyj fgf jhj ded kik sws lol aqa ;p;
GOOD WORK will lead to a HAPPY LIFE for you;
GOOD WORK will lead to a HAPPY LIFE for you;

aqa ;p; sws lol ded kik frf juj ftf jyj fgf jhj
The DAILY DRILLS will HELP YOU type with EASE;
The DAILY DRILLS will HELP YOU type with EASE;

frf juj ftf jyj fgf jhj ded kik sws lol aqa ;p;
GOOD SALARIES are USUALLY PAID to FAST TYPISTS;
GOOD SALARIES are USUALLY PAID to FAST TYPISTS;
```

LESSON 8

Aim: (a) To learn to use the **Full Stop Key**.
    (b) To learn to use the **Tabulator**.

1. Machine Adjustments: See Lesson 2.

2. Warm-up: (5 Minutes) Copy the first two lines exactly as shown; then throw the carriage twice and type the sentence 10 times—to strengthen your control of all the keys you have learned so far.

```
frf juj ftf jyj fgf jhj ded kik sws lol aqa ;p;
aqa ;p; sws lol ded kik frf juj ftf jyj fgf jhj
```

```
He will pay Jed Squire for the sugar this week;
```

3. New Key Control: (10 Minutes)

    (a) Learning to use the **Full Stop Key**.

    The L finger controls the **full stop key**.

Step 1—New Key Preview

Feel the centre of the **full stop key**—with the fingertip; then return the finger to the L key. Repeat this procedure several times—thinking of the L finger and the **full stop key** which it controls.

Step 2—New Key Try-out

Space twice after full stop at end of sentence.

```
. . . . . . 1.1 1.1 1.1 1.1 1.1 1.1 1.1 1.1 1.1
Hit it lightly.  Hit it lightly.  Hit it lightly.
Hit it lightly.  Hit it lightly.  Hit it lightly.
```

    (b) Learning to use the **Tabulator**.

    Your typewriter has a tabulator key or a tabulator bar with which you can make the carriage jump to any scale points you wish. (See Figs. 14, 15.)

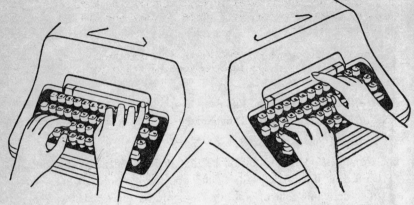

Fig. 14. Using the Tabulator Key.   **Fig. 15.** Using the Tabulator Bar.

Follow these steps for indenting paragraphs:

First: Remove **Tab Stops** already set.
  1. Move the carriage to the extreme left.
  2. Hold down the **clear** key and throw the carriage—to bring it back to the left margin.

Second: Set a **Tab Stop** 5 spaces from your left margin.
  1. Tap the space bar 5 times; then press the **Tab Set** key.
  2. Throw the carriage—to bring it back to the left margin.

Third: Tabulate.
  1. Hold down the Tabulator Key or the Tabulator Bar firmly with the finger nearest the key or bar—until the carriage stops.
  2. Your carriage is now at the paragraph beginning—5 spaces from the left margin.
  3. Practise returning the carriage to the left margin and using the tabulator until you can indent for a paragraph easily and quickly.

4. Self-Testing Work: (20 Minutes) Copy each paragraph **once**.
REMINDER: Space **twice** after a full stop that ends a sentence.

Throw carriage twice after each paragraph.

Strike all the keys with pep. Strike the keys
as though they were red hot. This is just how the
fast typist works.

Type with thought. Put forth your greatest
efforts. Let these two ideas guide you while you
type.

You should follow the daily drills as you are
told. These drills will show you that it is quite
easy to type well.

Start your daily work without delay. Keep at
it regularly. It is steady work that will take you
to your goal.

5. **Corrective Work:** (10 Minutes) Make a list of the words in which
   you find errors; then practise each word 3 times.

6. **Improvement Work:** (20 Minutes) Type another copy of the above
   4 paragraphs. Remember: Your aim in the **improvement work** is to
   turn out a **better job.** Now **relax** for a moment.

7. **Keyboard Review:** (10 Minutes) The following 8 lines will help you
   to strengthen your control of **F J R U.** Copy them exactly as shown.
   If you finish ahead of time, type them again—to see if you can turn
   out a **perfect** job.

Throw carriage twice after every second line.

```
for fat few fur foe fit fed fee for fat fir few fro;
fro few fir fat for fee fig foe fop fit fur fat fad;

jug jig jut jar joy jag jaw jar jet jot jog jug joy;
joy jug jog jag jaw joy jig jut jar jig jaw jog jet;

rye rut row red rip ray rap rug rig rut rye rug rot;
rot rye rut row red rip ray rap rug rig rut rye rug;

up us use uses urge ugly usage upper uproar upright;
us up use urge uses urge urges udder utters upstart;
```

LESSON 9

Aim: (*a*) To boost your typing skill by 1-minute timings.

(*b*) To learn to use the keys **V M**.

1. Machine Adjustments: See Lesson 2.

2. Warm-up: (5 Minutes) Copy the first two lines exactly as shown; then throw the carriage twice and type the sentence 10 times.

```
frf juj ftf jyj fgf jhj ded kik sws lol aqa ;p;
aqa ;p; sws lol ded kik frf juj ftf jyj fgf jhj

I will pay Joe Quig for the sugar today.
     1    2    3    4    5    6    7    8
```

NOTE (*a*) The above **warm-up** sentence contains 8 five-stroke words. A stroke means a letter, a space, or a punctuation mark.

(*b*) In calculating typing speed, 5 strokes count as 1 word.

3. Skill-Building Work: (10 Minutes) One good way to boost your skill is to type a sentence over and over, trying hard to improve each time you repeat it.

1-Minute Timed Test

Using a watch with a second hand, time yourself on the **warm-up** sentence above for 1 minute. If possible, ask a friend or a member of your family to time you.

Repeat the sentence as many times as you can before the end of the minute. Then—

(*a*) Jot down the number of words you typed and the number of errors you made.

(*b*) Subtract 1 for each error from the total words you typed. The answer shows the number of correct words you typed in 1 minute.

EXAMPLE: Assume that you typed 17 words and made 3 errors.

Total Words Typed...................................... 17

Subtract: (3 errors × 1)............................... −3

Correct Words Typed.................................. 14

(c) Take two more 1-minute timings. After each timing, see how many correct words you typed. Jot down the number.

(d) Now compare the results of all the 1-minute timings. See in which timing you typed the most **correct words.** That is your best score.

(e) Keep a Personal Progress Record of your best scores in the form of a table like the following sample:

1-Minute Timed Typing

Score Sheet

Lesson	Correct Words
9	14

TYPING TIP: *After each timing, practise the words in which you made errors until you can type them smoothly and accurately.*

4. New Key Control: (10 Minutes)

(a) Learning to use New Keys: **V M.**

V is controlled by the **F** finger.

M is controlled by the **J** finger.

Step 1—New Key Preview

Feel the centre of each new key—with the fingertip; then return the finger to its home base. Repeat this procedure several times. Think of the finger and the key it controls—to memorize the reach for the new keys.

Step 2—New Key Try-out

```
v v v v  fvf  fvf  fvf  fvf  m m m m  jmj  jmj  jmj  jmj
fvf  jmj  fvf  jmj  fvf  jmj  fvf  jmj  fvf  jmj  fvf  jmj
```

(b) Word Drill. Containing New Keys: **V M.**

```
vim vim vim vim vim vim met met met met met met
vim vim vim vim vim vim met met met met met met
```

5. Self-Testing Work: (25 Minutes) Part 1. Words and sentences. Copy the following 8 lines exactly as shown.

REMINDER: Space once after a semicolon.

```
over over over; gave gave gave; have have have;
home home home; seem seem seem; time time time;

ever ever ever; more more more; item item item;
live live live; vast vast vast; five five five;

You must devote more time to your daily work.
You must devote more time to your daily work.

You should go over every item with more thought.
You should go over every item with more thought.
```

Part 2. Paragraph Practice. Copy each paragraph ONCE.

1st: Remove all stops

2nd: Set a Tab Stop: For **Pica** type......................... at 20.

For **Elite** type .... at 30.

3rd: Set Line Space Gauge for **double** spacing

Double spacing has one blank line between typed lines.

REMINDER: Space twice after a full stop that ends a sentence.

```
You will surely make good if you give more time

to your daily work here.  You must make every effort

to make good.

    You will improve your skill every day if you

devote some thought to your work.  You will surely

progress if you keep at your work regularly.  Just

have faith.

    Skilful typists command very good salaries.  All

types of firms require them.  So try your utmost to

develop your skill.
```

6. Corrective Works: (10 Minutes) Make a list of the words in which you find errors; then practise each word 3 times.

7. Improvement Work: (10 Minutes) Type another copy of the same 3 paragraphs. Try for smoother and more accurate typing.

8. Challenge Work: (5 Minutes) Another challenge to you! Here are 8 new lines containing the letters **G H T Y** . . . to test your mastery of them. See if you can turn out a **perfect** copy.

Set Line Space Gauge for single spacing.
Throw the carriage twice after every second line.

```
go got get gas gag gap gay gig gray greed great;
go gig gay gap gas gag get gas gray great greed;

her has had his hit hot hut hat hay hag had his;
his had hag hay hat hut hot hit his had has her;

to try tip tap two tag too to try tip tap two;
to two tap tip try too try to top tap tag try;

you yes yet yap yell year yoke your yowl yore;
yap yet yes you yore yowl your yoke year yell;
```

LESSON 10

Aim: (*a*) To boost your typing skill by 1-minute timings.

(*b*) To learn to use the keys **B N**.

1. Machine Adjustments: See Lesson 2.

2. Warm-up: (5 Minutes) Copy the first two lines exactly as shown; then throw the carriage twice and type the sentence 10 times:

```
frf juj ftf jyj fgf jhj ded kik sws lol aqa ;p;
fgf jhj fvf jmj fgf jhj fvf jmj fgf jhj fvf jmj
```

```
Paul Quigs will devote more time to his work.
```

```
    1   2   3   4   5   6   7   8   9
```

5 strokes count as 1 *word.*

3. Skill-Building Work: (10 Minutes) As in Lesson 9, take three 1-minute timings on the **warm-up** sentence. Repeat it as many times as you can before the end of the minute. Enter it in your Personal Progress Record—the 1-Minute Timed Typing Score Sheet which you established in Lesson 9.

REMINDER: After each timing, practise the words in which you made errors until you can type them smoothly and accurately.

4. New Key Control: (10 Minutes) Learning to use **B N**.

B is controlled by the **F** finger.

N is controlled by the **J** finger.

Step 1—New Key Preview

Feel the centre of each new key—with the fingertip; then return the finger quickly to its home base. Repeat this fingering several times. Think of the finger and the key it controls—to memorize the new key location.

Step 2—New Key Try-out

```
b b b b fbf fbf fbf fbf n n n n jnj jnj jnj jnj
fbf jnj fbf jnj fbf jnj fbf jnj fbf jnj fbf jnj
```

Step 3—Word Drill

```
bin bin bin bin bin bin nib nib nib nib nib nib
big big big big big big now now now now now now
```

5. **Self-Testing Work:** (25 Minutes) Part 1. Words and Sentences. Copy the following 8 lines exactly as shown:

Aim for Accuracy.

```
bun bun bun; nip nip nip; fib fib fib; win win win;
fib fib fib; win win win; bun bun bun; nip nip nip;

bent bent bent; nine nine nine; vent vent vent;
mend mend mend; vine vine vine; blow blow blow;

We require more time to turn out a very good job.
We require more time to turn out a very good job.

Be prompt. Never shirk. Make promptness a habit.
Be prompt. Never shirk. Make promptness a habit.
```

Part 2. Paragraph Practice.

Step 1. Remove all stops.

Step 2. Set Tab Stops: For **Pica** type......................... at 20.
For **Elite** type .... at 30.

Step 3. Set Line Space Gauge for **double** spacing.
Copy each paragraph **once**.

Your machine is now set for double spacing.
Throw carriage once after each line and after each paragraph.

REMINDER: Space twice after a colon.

```
Never put off until tomorrow any job you should

finish today.  Try to be prompt at all times.  No one

likes to be kept waiting.
```

    Keep on working just as diligently as you have

been doing up to this point. You will soon be a

master of the keyboard. You will have a valuable

skill that will repay you for your efforts.

    Remember this: everybody is able to learn

typing. All they have to do is to put forth their

very best efforts. This means thinking while training

every finger to strike the right key.

6. Corrective Work: (10 Minutes) Make a list of the words in which you find errors; then practise each word 3 times.

7. Improvement Work: (10 Minutes) Try the first two paragraphs again. See if you can type the first one **perfectly.**

8. Challenge Work: (5 Minutes) The following 8 lines give you a good review of the letters **D E K I.** Challenge yourself to turn out a **perfect copy.**

Keep your eyes here. Every line is different

```
do dot due dye day dew dab den dim dog die dig dry dip
do dig dry dip die dog dim dab den dew day dye due dot

ebb eke err eve end egg ever even edge earn east evil
err eke eve end ebb eel evil east earn edge envy easy

kid kin kit keg key king kind know knee knot knew
key keg kid kit kin knew knot knee knob king kind

it is in if ire ill ink inn imp idle item isle iron
if in is it imp inn ill ire ink item idle iron isle
```

LESSON 11

Aim: (*a*) To boost your typing skill by 1-minute timings.

(*b*) To learn to use **C** , (Comma).

1. Machine Adjustments: See Lesson 2.

2. Warm-up: (5 Minutes) Copy the first two lines exactly as shown; then throw the carriage twice and type the sentence 10 times.

```
frf juj ftf jyj fgf jhj ded kik sws lol aqa ;p;
fvf jmj fbf jnj fvf jmj fbf jnj fvf jmj fbf jnj
```

```
The Ben Mavis firm submitted the lowest quotation.
    1    2    3    4    5    6    7    8    9    10
```

3. Skill-Building Work: (10 Minutes) As before, take three 1-minute timings on the **warm-up** sentence. Repeat it as many times as you can before the end of the minute.

4. New Key Control: (10 Minutes) Learning to use New Keys: **C** and , (Comma).

C is controlled by the **D** finger.

, is controlled by the **K** finger.

Step 1—New Key Preview

Feel the centre of each new key—with the fingertip; then return the finger quickly to its home base. Repeat this fingering several times—thinking of the finger and the key it controls.

Step 2—New Key Try-out

Strike comma lightly.

```
c c c c dcd dcd dcd dcd , , , , k,k k,k k,k k,k
dcd k,k dcd k,k dcd k,k dcd k,k dcd k,k dcd k,k
```

37

Step 3—Word Drill

```
can, can, can, can, can, cue, cue, cue, cue, cue,
can, can, can, can, can, cue, cue, cue, cue, cue,
```

5. Self-Testing Work: (30 Minutes) Part 1. Words and Sentences. Copy the following 10 lines exactly as shown:

TYPING RULE: Space once after a comma.

```
cash, cash, cash, lack, lack, lack, lace, lace, lace,
lack, lack, lack, lace, lace, lace, cash, cash, cash,

could, could, could, clerk, clerk, clerk, camp, camp,
clerk, clerk, clerk, could, could, could, cane, cane,

If you call before three, the bank will cash your cheque.
If you call before three, the bank will cash your cheque.

Charles Condon, sales manager, was in complete charge.
Charles Condon, sales manager, was in complete charge.

He may, if convenient, have it charged to his account.
He may, if convenient, have it charged to his account.
```

Part 2. Paragraph Practice.

Step 1. Remove all stops.

Step 2. Set Tab Stops: For **Pica** type.......................... at 20.
For **Elite** type .... at 30.

Step 3. Set Line Space Gauge for **double** spacing.

Copy each paragraph **once**.
Keep wrists low but not touching the machine. Return to guide keys quickly.

```
     Space once after a comma.  Space once after a

semicolon.  Space twice after a full stop that ends

a sentence.  Strike each key with the same force.

     The tabulator is a device which helps you to
```

```
type faster.  It enables you to skip across the page

to any point you desire.

     First, set a tab stop at the point to which you

wish the carriage to jump.  Second, move the carriage

back to the left margin.  Third, hold the tabulator

bar or the tabulator key down until the carriage has

stopped.
```

6. Corrective Work: (10 Minutes) Make a list of the words in which you find errors; then practise each word 3 times.

REMINDER: When you hear the bell, finish the word you are typing and throw the carriage for the next line.

7. Improvement Work: (15 Minutes) Now relax a moment. Then type another copy of the above 3 paragraphs. This time try to type them more smoothly and more accurately. Try for real improvement.

8. Challenge Work: (5 Minutes) The following 8 lines test your mastery of **S W L O**. Challenge yourself to a **perfect** copy.

Keep your eyes here.

```
sub sum see sun set sit sin sip she ship shall shame
sit sin sip set sub sum see sod sob slip sweep super

won win who why wet was weak wear west well what when
was wet why who win won what well wear west when what

lad lid lot let log lie lag lug lip last late lawn
lip lag lug lie log let lot lid lad land lane last

own out owl old one oak out oil off over oven open
off oil out oak one old owl our own open ours over
```

LESSON 12

Aim: (*a*) To boost your typing skill by 2-minute timings.
      (*b*) To learn to use **X** and to review the **full stop key.**

1. Machine Adjustments: See Lesson 2.

2. Warm-up: (5 Minutes) Copy the first two lines exactly as shown;
then throw the carriage twice and type the sentence 10 times.

```
frf juj ftf jyj fgf jhj fvf jmj fbf jnj fvf jmj
ded kik sws lol aqa ;p; dod k,k dod k,k fvf jmj

Mona and Bert are making plans for their holiday.
```

3. Skill-Building Work: (15 Minutes) This consists of:
      (*a*) Preview Practice on Words and Phrases ....   3 minutes
      (*b*) Three 2-Minute Timings and Word Practice.........12 minutes
                                                           ——
                                                       15 minutes

    First: **Preview Practice.** To prepare yourself for the 2-minute
              timings, practise each of the following words and phrases
              3 times:

```
touch...learn...above...typing...talent...
average...special...that is...You do......
You do not
```

Second: **Machine Adjustments.**
        (*a*) Remove all tab stops.
        (*b*) Set a Tab Stop 5 spaces from your left margin.
        (*c*) Set Line Space Gauge for **double** spacing.

 Third: **Three 2-Minute Timings.**
        Time yourself for 2 minutes on the following paragraph. Re-
        peat it if you finish before the end of 2 minutes.
                    Figures indicate number of 5-stroke words.

40

```
                          5
    Touch typing is easy to learn.  You do not need
 10                        15
a mind that is above the average.  You do not even
 20                        25  26
need a special talent for typing.
```

Fourth: **Calculate Your Typing Speed—after each timing.**

     (*a*) Jot down the total words typed and the total errors made.

     (*b*) Subtract 1 for each error from the total words typed.

     (*c*) Divide the remainder by 2—because you typed for 2 minutes. The result indicates your typing speed in correct words per minute.

> EXAMPLE: Assume that in the first 2-minute timing, you typed 29 words with 4 errors.
>
> | | |
> |---|---:|
> | Total Words Typed .... | 29 |
> | Subtract: (4 errors × 1) .... | −4 |
> | Correct Words Typed .... | 2/25 |
> | Correct Words Per Minute .... | 12½ |
>
> Your typing speed in correct words is 13 words per minute.

> NOTE: (*a*) Fractions ½ and over are counted as whole numbers.
>
>   (*b*) Fractions less than ½ are dropped.

   (*d*) See in which timing you typed the most correct words. Consider that your best 2-minute score.

> EXAMPLE: Assume that the three 2-minute timings which you have taken show the following results:
>
> | *Timing* | *Correct Words Typed* |
> |---|:---:|
> | 1st .... | 13 |
> | 2nd .... | 15 |
> | 3rd........................... | 14 |
>
> Your best score is in the second timing—because you typed the most correct words.

REMINDER: After each timing, practise the words in which you made errors until you can type them smoothly and accurately.

4. New Key Control: (10 Minutes) Learning to use **X** and . (Full stop).
X is controlled by the S finger.
. is controlled by the L finger.

Step 1—New Key Preview

Feel the centre of each new key—with the fingertip; then return the finger quickly to its home base. Repeat this fingering several times—thinking of the finger and the key it controls—to memorize the new key location.

Step 2—New Key Try-out

Strike full stop lightly.

```
x x x x sxs sxs sxs sxs . . . . 1.1 1.1 1.1 1.1
sxs 1.1 sxs 1.1 sxs 1.1 sxs 1.1 sxs 1.1 sxs 1.1
```

Step 3—Word Drill

Space once after an abbreviation.

```
six six six six six six etc. etc. etc. etc. etc.
six six six six six six etc. etc. etc. etc. etc.
```

5. Self-Testing Work: (25 Minutes)
Part 1. Words and Sentences.
Copy the following 8 lines. **Single** spacing.

```
fixes fixes fixes; mixes mixes mixes; taxes taxes;
mixes mixes mixes; fixes fixes fixes; boxes boxes;

expert expert expert; expect expect expect; excels;
exceed exceed exceed; excuse excuse excuse; excels;

Dr. Lux, tax expert, will examine the tax returns.
Dr. Lux, tax expert, will examine the tax returns.
```

```
Mr. Cox examined the mixture with extreme care.
Mr. Cox examined the mixture with extreme care.
```

Part 2. Paragraph Practice.

Step 1. Remove all stops.

Step 2. Set Tab Stops: For **Pica** type........................ at 20.
For **Elite** type .... at 30.

Step 3. Set Line Space Gauge for **double** spacing.
Copy each paragraph **once**.

Space once after an abbreviation.

```
    Mr. Roxbury and Mr. Saxton will examine the six

boxes of wax with extreme care.  These boxes were

returned by Prof. Maxton of Knoxville College.

    The Government tax experts were exceedingly

careful in examining the current tax receipts.  The

amount showed an excess of six million pounds over

the previous year.

    Sixteen boxes of explosives were packed with the

most extreme care and shipped by Fox Express Company.

These explosives are to be used in secret experiments

for the British Government.
```

6. Corrective Work: (10 Minutes) Make a list of the words in which you find errors; then practise each word 3 times.

7. Improvement Work: (10 Minutes) Try another copy of the above 3 paragraphs—for real improvement.

8. Challenge Work: (5 Minutes) The following 6 lines test your control of **A Q ; P**. See if you can turn out a **perfect** copy.

act ant and ask apt any art all age able acid aged
age all art any ask act add axe ant aged able acid

quit quip quote quite queer queen quack quaint quorum
quip quit quite quote queen queer quail quorum quaint

pin pup put; pull palm pant; pint pile push; punch;
put pin pup; pant pull palm; push pick pile; paper;

LESSON 13

Aim: (a) To boost your typing skill by 3-minute timings.

(b) To learn to use **Z** and ½ (One half).

1. Machine Adjustments: See Lesson 2.

2. Warm-up: (5 Minutes) Copy the first two lines exactly as shown; then throw the carriage twice and type the sentence 10 times.

```
frf juj ftf jyj fgf jhj ded kik sws lol aqa ;p;
fvf jmj fbf jnj dcd k,k sxs 1.1 dcd k,k sxs 1.1
```

```
To become an expert typist, you must practise each day.
```

3. Skill-Building Work: (20 Minutes) This consists of:

(a) Preview Practice on Words and Phrases .... 5 minutes

(b) Three 3-Minute Timings and Word Practice ...... 15 minutes

                                                                  ——

                                                        20 minutes

First: **Preview Practice:** To prepare yourself for the 3-minute test, practise each of the following words and phrases three times:

REMINDER: When bell rings, finish the word and throw carriage for new line.

```
touch...learn...above...typing...talent...average
special...lessons...you do...for you...is the
do the...of the...in this
```

Second: **Machine Adjustments.**

(a) Remove all tab stops.

(b) Set a Tab Stop 5 spaces from your left margin.

(c) Set Line Space Gauge for **double** spacing.

Third: **Three 3-Minute Timings.**

Time yourself for 3 minutes on the following paragraphs. Repeat them if you finish before the end of 3 minutes.

45

<pre>
                            5
     Touch typing is easy to learn. You do not need
  10   15
a mind that is above the average. You do not even
  20   25
need a special talent for typing.
                         30   35
     All you need is the will to learn. The lessons
                      40   45
in this book do the rest of the job for you; they
                      50   53
make touch typing easy for you to learn.
</pre>

Fourth: **Calculate Your Typing Speed—after each timing.**

      (*a*) Jot down the total words typed and the total errors made.

      (*b*) Subtract 1 for each error from the total words typed.

      (*c*) Divide the remainder by 3—because you typed for 3 minutes. The result indicates your typing speed in correct words per minute.

      EXAMPLE:

          Total Words Typed 48

          Subtract: (4 Errors × 1) .... −4

          Correct Words Typed....................................3/44

          Correct Words Per Minute .... $14\frac{2}{3}$

      Your typing speed in correct words is 15 words a minute. Fractions $\frac{1}{2}$ and over are counted as whole numbers.

      (*d*) See in which timing you typed the most correct words per minute. Consider that your best score.

Assume that the 3 three-minute timings which you have taken show the following results:

Timing	Correct Words Typed Per Minute
1st	15
2nd	17
3rd	16

Your best score is in the second timing—because you typed the most correct words per minute.

REMINDER: After each timing, practise the words in which you made
errors.

4. New Key Control: (10 Minutes) Learning to use New Keys: **Z** and
½ (One half)
    Z is controlled by the **A** finger.
    ½ is controlled by the **;** finger.

Step 1—New Key Preview

Feel the centre of each new key—with the fingertip; then return the
finger quickly to its home base. Repeat this fingering several times—
thinking of the finger and the key it controls—to memorize the new
key location.

Step 2—New Key Try-out

Keep elbows close to body.

aqa ;p; aza ;½; qaz p;½ zaq ½;p

Step 3—Word Drill

power apply piece plain reply topaz
azure equal about quart amaze apart

5. Self-Testing Work: (25 Minutes) Part 1. Words and Sentences. Copy
the following 8 lines as shown:

zest zest zest; lazy lazy lazy; size size size; zeal;
zero zero zero; zest zest zest; lazy lazy lazy; zeal;

blaze blaze blaze; amaze amaze amaze; zebra zebra;
dizzy dizzy dizzy; blaze blaze blaze; amaze amaze;

The lazy zebra at the zoo quickly drank the mixture.
The lazy zebra at the zoo quickly drank the mixture.

Ship five boxes of zinc trays by Zale Express.
Ship five boxes of zinc trays by Zale Express.

Part 2. Paragraph Practice. Copy the following 3 paragraphs **once**. **Double** spacing.

    If you work with zeal and zest, you will soon be
a competent typist. The ability to type well is a
very valuable asset.

    You can develop your typing skill quickly by the
proper habits of work. You should realize that poor
work is a mere waste of time. Try to be exact.

    Every business firm is dependent on the services
of competent typists. You are now equipping yourself
with a skill for which there is a constant demand.

6. Corrective Work: (10 Minutes) Make a list of the words containing errors; then practise each word 3 times.

7. Challenge Work: (5 Minutes) The following 8 lines test your control of **B N V M.** See if you can turn out a **perfect** job.

Return to guide keys quickly.

    bag big bug bit bud bed bid bun bale bend bank bask
    but bid bed bun bid big bag bud bask bale band bank

    not now nut nor note nose none nude noun nine nest
    now not nor nut nose note nude none nine nest next

    vim vet van vex vet vast vote veto vase vine vial
    van vex vet vim vex vial vine vase veto vote vast

    man mix mat mad made mail main make mark mask mine
    mad met mix men mask mark made main male made mint

LESSON 14

Aim: (*a*) To boost your typing skill by 4-minute timings.
(*b*) To learn to use the **?** (Question Mark).

1. Machine Adjustments: See Lesson 2.

2. Warm-up: (5 Minutes) Copy the first two lines exactly as shown; then throw the carriage twice and type the sentence ten times.

```
frf juj ftf jyj fgf jhj ded kik sws lol aqa ;p;
fvf jmj fbf jnj dcd k,k sxs 1.1 aza ;½; aza ;½;

Liza quickly mixed the very big jar of new soap.
```

3. Skill-Building Work: (20 Minutes)
(*a*) Preview Practice on Words and Phrases .... 3 minutes
(*b*) Three 4-Minute Timings and Word Practice.........17 minutes
—
20 minutes

First: **Preview Practice.** To prepare yourself for the 4-minute timings, practise each of the following words and phrases 3 times:

```
touch...learn...above...aside...typing
talent...amount...average...special
lessons...definite...is the...of the
for you...you do...that is...in this
you do not
```

Second: **Machine Adjustments.**
(*a*) Remove all tab stops.
(*b*) Set a Tab Stop 5 spaces from your left margin.
(*c*) Set Line Space Gauge for **double** spacing.

Third: **Three 4-Minute Timings.**
Time yourself for 4 minutes on the following paragraphs, repeating the copy until the end of 4 minutes.

```
                          5
      Touch typing is easy to learn.  You do not need
  10                      15
a mind that is above the average.  You do not even
  20                      25
need a special talent for typing.
                          30                      35
      All you need is the will to learn.  The lessons
                          40                      45
in this book do the rest of the job for you; they
                          50
make touch typing easy for you to learn.
          55                      60
      Try to set aside each day a definite amount of
          65          67
time for each lesson.
```

Fourth: **Calculate Your Typing Speed—after each timing.**

        (*a*) Jot down the total words typed and the total errors made.

        (*b*) Subtract 1 for each error from the total words typed.

        (*c*) Divide the remainder by 4—because you typed for 4 minutes. The result indicates your typing speed in correct words per minute.

    REMINDER: After each timing, practise the words in which you made errors.

4. New Key Control: (5 Minutes) Learning to use the Question Mark. The Question Mark is controlled by the **K** finger.

Step 1—New Key Preview

    1st: Hold down the left shift key.

    2nd: Reach for the Question Mark key.

    3rd: Return fingers to home base.

    4th: Repeat this several times until you develop smoothness in shifting and reaching for the Question Mark.

Step 2—New Key Try-out

Space twice after a Question Mark.

```
? ? ? ? ? ? Who?   Who?   Who?   Who?   Who?   Who?
? ? ? ? ? ? Why?   Why?   Why?   Why?   Why?   Why?
```

5. Self-Testing Work: (30 Minutes) Part 1. Sentence Practice. Copy the following ten lines exactly as shown.

Keep your eyes on the copy.
Every line is different.

```
How much?   How many?   How soon?   How early?   How fast?
How many?   How much?   How fast?   How large?   How soon?

Where is Max?   Where is Mary?   What is Cora sewing?
Where is Sam?   Where is Paul?   What is Zeke fixing?

Can Max swim?   Can he dance?   Can he play tennis?
Can he dance?   Does he swim?   Do you like tennis?

Did you open the mail?   Did you read the note?
Did you read the note?   Did you open the mail?

Can Van do the work?   Will he require aid?   Who knows?
Can Jim complete it?   Is he quite capable?   Who knows?
```

Part 2. Paragraph Practice. Copy the following 4 paragraphs once. **Double** spacing.

Space twice after a Question Mark.
Throw carriage once after each line.

```
Do you set aside a definite amount of time each

day for practice?  Do you start work promptly?  Can

you make the various machine adjustments quickly?

Do you keep your fingers curved?  Do you strike

each key sharply with the tip of the finger?  Do you

keep your eyes on the copy?

Do you throw the carriage without looking up?

Do you keep your right hand on the home keys when

you throw the carriage?  Do you use the paper release

to remove your paper?
```

Do you practise the words in which you made

errors? Do you practise them as explained in this

book? Do you follow the instructions exactly as given?

6. **Corrective Work:** (10 Minutes) Make a list of the words in which you find errors; then practise each one until you can type it smoothly and accurately.

7. **Challenge Work:** (5 Minutes) The following 4 lines test your control of the letters **X** and **Z**. Challenge yourself to turn out two **perfect** copies!

Think of the finger and the key it controls.

```
lax vex six tax fix taxed fixing mixing taxing vexing
fix tax vex lax six fixed vexing taxing fixing mixing

zip zoo zest zeal zinc zero lazy zone zoom zinc zealot
zoo zip zoom zone lazy zinc zeal zest zero zone zealot
```

LESSON 15

Aim: (*a*) To boost your typing skill by 5-minute timings.
(*b*) To learn to use the figures **1, 4, 7.**

1. Machine Adjustments: See Lesson 2.

2. Warm-up: (5 Minutes) Copy the first two lines exactly as shown; then throw the carriage twice and type the sentence 10 times.

```
frf juj ftf jyj fgf jhj ded kik sws lol aqa ;p;
fvf jmj fbf jnj dcd k,k sxs 1.1 aza ;½; aza ;½;
```

```
Pack my box with seventy two jugs of liquid veneer.
```

3. Skill-Building Work: (20 Minutes)
    (*a*) Preview Practice on Words and Phrases .... 3 minutes
    (*b*) Two 1-Minute Timings and Word Practice .... 3 minutes
    (*c*) Two 5-Minute Timings and Word Practice ....14 minutes
                                                  ——
                                              20 minutes

First: Preview Practice. To prepare yourself for the 1-minute and 5-minute timings, practise each of the following words and phrases 3 times:

```
touch...learn...above...aside...typing
talent...amount...follow...easily...become
typist...average...special...lessons...definite
exactly...quickly...surprised...is the...
of the...in the...in this...for you
you will...you will be
```

Second: Machine Adjustments.
    (*a*) Remove all tab stops.
    (*b*) Set a Tab Stop 5 spaces from left margin.
    (*c*) Set Line Space Gauge for **double** spacing.

Third: **Two 1-Minute Timings.**

Take two 1-minute tests on the following paragraph. Repeat the copy if you finish before the end of the minute. This is a Warm-up for the 5-minute timing.

                            5
```
    Touch typing is easy to learn.  You do not need
10                        15
a mind that is above the average.  You do not even
20                        25  26
need a special talent for typing.
```

Fourth: **Calculate Your Typing Speed—after each timing.**

(*a*) Jot down the total words typed.

(*b*) Subtract 1 for each error. The result indicates your typing speed in correct words per minute.

(*c*) See in which timing you typed the most correct words. That is your best score. Enter it in your Personal Progress Record of 1-Minute Timings shown in Lesson 9.

Fifth: **Two 5-Minute Timings.** Relax a while; then take two 5-minute tests on the copy below. Repeat if you finish before end of 5 minutes. Try to maintain your best 1-minute rate.

                            5
```
    Touch typing is easy to learn.  You do not need
10                        15
a mind that is above the average.  You do not even
20                        25
need a special talent for typing.
                      30                        35
    All you need is the will to learn.  The lessons
                  40                        45
in this book do the rest of the job for you; they
                  50
make touch typing easy for you to learn.
            55                        60
    Try to set aside each day a definite amount of
            65                        70
time for each lesson.  Follow each step in the lesson
      75                        80
exactly as given.  You will be surprised how easily
            85                        90    92
and quickly you will become a touch typist.
```

Sixth: **Calculate Your Typing Speed—after each timing.**

(*a*) Jot down the total words typed and the total errors made.

(*b*) Subtract 1 for each error from the total words typed.

(*c*) Divide the remainder by 5—because you typed for 5 minutes. The result shows your typing speed in correct words per minute.

REMINDER: Practice the words in which you made errors—after each timing.

4. **New Key Control:** (10 Minutes) Learning to use figures **1, 4, 7.**
Strike small l for the number 1.
Figure **1** is controlled by the **L** finger.
Figure **4** is controlled by the **F** finger.
Figure **7** is controlled by the **J** finger.

Step 1—New Key Preview

Feel the centre of each new key—with the fingertip; then return the finger quickly to its home base. Repeat this fingering several times—thinking of the finger and the key it controls.

Step 2—New Key Try-out

Return finger quickly to home base.

```
f4f f4f f4f f4f f4f f4f j7j j7j j7j j7j j7j j7j
f4f j7j f4f j7j f4f j7j f4f j7j f4f j7j f4f j7j

or 4 or 4 or 4 ru 7 ru 7 ru 7 or 4 ru 7 or 4 ru 7
or 4 ru 7 or 4 ru 7 or 4 ru 7 or 4 ru 7 or 4 ru 7
```

5. **Self-Testing Works** (25 Minutes) Part 1. Words and Sentences. Copy the following 10 lines exactly as shown:

Strike small l for the number one. Space once after an abbreviation.

```
June 1; July 4; April 7; January 4; March 17, 1741
July 4; June 1; March 4; October 7; April 14, 1471

What is the sum of 11 and 7 and 4 and 1 and 714?
What is the sum of 17 and 4 and 7 and 1 and 174?
```

```
Florence is 7 years 11 months and 17 days old today.
Veronica is 4 years 11 months and 14 days old today.

Your order of November 14 was shipped on December 17.
Your order of December 11 was shipped on February 14.

Policy No. 141174 will expire on Monday, November 14.
Policy No. 471714 will expire on Friday, December 17.
```

Part 2. Paragraph Practice. **Double Spacing.** Copy each paragraph
once.

```
Captain James Cook, the English explorer, was born

in the village of Marton in Yorkshire.  He proclaimed

New South Wales a British possession in 1770.

In 1741, a notable Frenchman, Joseph Francois Dupleix,

became Governor of Pondicherry.  He began to train

native troops, and to enter into alliances with native

chiefs.
```

6. Corrective Work: (5 Minutes) As usual.

7. Improvement Work: (10 Minutes) Try the 2 paragraphs again. See if
you can type at least 1 of them **perfectly.**

LESSON 16

Aim: (*a*) To develop sustained skill by 5-Minute Timings.

(*b*) To learn to use the figures **5** and **6**.

1. Machine Adjustments: See Lesson 2.

2. Warm-up: (5 Minutes) Copy the first two lines exactly as shown; then throw the carriage and type the sentence 10 times.

Strike small l for number one.

```
frf f4f juj j7j frf f4f juj j7j f4f j7j f4f j7j
1 4 1 7 1 4 1 7 174 4 1 7 1 471 147 471 714 417
```

Queen Anne granted that patent on January 7, 1714.

3. Skill-Building Work: (20 Minutes)

(*a*) Preview Practice on Words and Phrases .... 3 minutes

(*b*) Two 1-Minute Timings and Word Practice .... 3 minutes

(*c*) Two 5-Minute Timings and Word Practice ....14 minutes

$\overline{}$ 20 minutes

First: **Preview Practice.** Practise the following words and phrases 3 times each:

```
erase...strike...margin...utmost...typing...
another...correct...teacher...previous...
training...attractive...will be...in your...
in which...You have
```

Second: **Machine Adjustments.**

(*a*) Remove all tab stops.

(*b*) Set a Tab Stop 5 spaces from left margin.

(*c*) Set Line Space Gauge for **double** spacing.

Third: **Two 1-Minute Timings.** Take two 1-minute tests on the following paragraph. Repeat the copy if you finish before end of minute. This is a Warm-up for the 5-minute timing.

57

```
               5
    Do not erase.  Do not cross out.  Do not strike
  10                        15
one letter over another.  Let your errors stand.
    20                    24
Finish every line you start.
```

Fourth: (*a*) Calculate your speed in correct words in each timing.

(*b*) Enter the better of the two timings in your Personal Progress Record.

(*c*) Practise the words in which you made errors—after each timing.

Fifth: **Two 5-Minute Timings.** Relax a while; then take two 5-minute timings on the copy following. Repeat if you finish before end of 5 minutes. Try to maintain your best 1-minute rate.

```
               5
    Do not erase.  Do not cross out.  Do not strike
  10                        15
one letter over another.  Let your errors stand.
    20
Finish every line you start.
        25                        30
    You correct your typing errors by practising the
  35                        40
words in which you made errors.  You have been doing
  45                        50
this in the previous lessons.  Keep on doing so.
  55                        60
That is the best practice for training your fingers
  65
to strike the right keys.
        70                        75
    Try your utmost to turn out attractive work.
        80              83
Take pride in your typing.
```

Sixth: (*a*) Calculate your speed in correct words per minute.

(*b*) Enter the better of the two results in your Personal Progress Record.

4. New Key Control: (10 Minutes) Learning to use the figures **5** and **6**.

Figure **5** is controlled by the **F** finger.

Figure **6** is controlled by the **J** finger.

Step 1—New Key Preview

Reach and touch the centre of each new key—with the fingertip; then
return the finger quickly to its home base. Repeat this fingering
several times—thinking of the finger and the key it controls—to
memorize the new key location.

Step 2—New Key Try-out

Strike sharply, Return finger quickly to home base

```
f5f  f5f  f5f  f5f  f5f  f5f  j6j  j6j  j6j  j6j  j6j  j6j
f5f  j6j  f5f  j6j  f5f  j6j  f5f  j6j  f5f  j6j  f5f  j6j

if 5 by 6 if 5 by 6 if 5 by 6 if 5 by 6 if 5 by 6
if 5 by 6 if 5 by 6 if 5 by 6 if 5 by 6 if 5 by 6
```

5. Self-Testing Work: (30 Minutes) Part 1. Sentence Practice. Copy the
following 12 lines exactly as shown. **Single** spacing.

> *Space once after an abbreviation.*
> *Throw carriage twice after every third line.*
> *Throw the carriage with a flip of the wrist.*

```
f4f  j7j  f5f  j6j  f4f  j7j  f5f  j6j  f4f  j7j  f5f  j6j
15 kg coffee; 16 eggs; 56 boxes oranges;
65 kg coffee; 14 eggs; 75 boxes oranges;

or 4 ru 7 it 5 my 6 or 4 ru 7 it 5 my 6 147 156
The Barton Market is at 516 West 147th Street.
The Baxter Market is at 165 East 165th Street.

fr4 ju7 ft5 jy6 f4f j7j f5f j6j f4f j7j f5f j6j
Robert Fulton was born in Pennsylvania in 1765.
William Penn, English Quaker, was born in 1644.

or 4 ru 7 it 5 by 6 or 4 ru 7 it 5 by 6 174 516
The sum of 15 and 51 and 65 and 41 and 475 is 647.
The sum of 51 and 15 and 56 and 14 and 475 is 611.
```

Part 2. Paragraph Practice. **Double** spacing. Copy each paragraph **once.**

```
On June 15, 1775, George Washington was elected
```

```
by Congress the Chief Commander of the American forces.
```

He scored a brilliant victory at Trenton on Christmas

night, 1776.

The Declaration of Independence, a famous state

paper, was issued by the American Continental Congress

on July 4, 1776. It was drawn up by Thomas Jefferson.

The invasion fleet consisted of 4 battleships, 15

light cruisers, 6 aircraft carriers, 17 troopships, and

5 submarines. Air protection consisted of 14 bombers,

175 fighters, 6 helicopters, and 75 paratroop planes.

6. Corrective Work: (5 Minutes) Make a list of the words in which you find errors; then practise each word 3 times.

Thoughtful practice leads to accuracy.

7. Challenge Work: (5 Minutes) The last paragraph above contains all the figures you have learned so far. See if you can turn out a **perfect** copy.

LESSON 17

Aim: (*a*) To develop sustained typing skill by 5-minute timings.

(*b*) To learn to use the figures **3** and **8**.

1. Machine Adjustments: See Lesson 2.

2. Warm-up: (5 Minutes) Copy the first two lines exactly as shown; then throw the carriage twice and type the sentence 10 times.

```
f4f j7j f5f j6j f4f j7j f5f j6j f4f j7j f5f j6j
417 147 517 157 617 167 617 171 714 471 651 174

The sum of 14 and 57 and 67 and 11 and 5 equals 154.
```

3. Skill-Building Work: (20 Minutes)

(*a*) Preview Practice on Words and Phrases .... 3 minutes

(*b*) Two 1-Minute Timings and Word Practice .... 3 minutes

(*c*) Two 5-Minute Timings and Word Practice ....14 minutes

—

20 minutes

First: **Preview Practice:** Practise each of the following words and phrases 3 times.

```
never...typing...office...become...getting...
acquire...efforts...valuable...personal...
possible...business...shorthand...it is...
it can...to it...in the...to use...to have
if you...from you...why not
```

Second: **Machine Adjustments:**

(*a*) Remove all tab stops.

(*b*) Set a Tab Stop 5 spaces from left margin.

(*c*) Set Line Space Gauge for **double** spacing.

Third: **Take two 1-minute timings on the following paragraph:**

5
Typing is a very valuable skill to acquire. It
10   15   20
is valuable for personal use and as a means of getting
                    23
an office job.

> REMINDER: (*a*) See in which timing you typed the most
> correct words. That is your best score.
> Enter it in your Personal Progress Record
> —the 1-Minute Timed Typing Score Sheet
> you established in Lesson 9.
>
> (*b*) Practise the words in which you made
> errors—after each timing.

Fourth: **Two 5-Minute Timings.** Relax a while; then take two 5-minute
timings on the copy below. Repeat if you finish before end of
5 minutes. Try to maintain your best 1-minute rate.

5
Typing is a very valuable skill to acquire. It
10   15   20
is valuable for personal use and as a means of getting
                    25   30
an office job. This skill is yours to use; it can
                    35
never be taken from you.
                              40
So why not put forth your best efforts to become
45   50
a good typist. You can become a good typist if you
55   60   65
put your mind to it. You should also, if possible,
                    70   75
learn shorthand. Typing and shorthand are two very
                    80
valuable skills to have.
                              85
These two skills will help you get a good start
90   94
in the business world.

> REMINDER: Enter your best 5-Minute score in your Per-
> sonal Progress Record.

4. New Key Control: (10 Minutes) Learning to use the Figures **3** and **8**.
Figure **3** is controlled by the **D** finger.
Figure **8** is controlled by the **K** finger.

Step 1—New Key Preview

Reach and touch the centre of each new key—with the fingertip; then
return the finger quickly to its home base. Repeat this fingering
several times—thinking of the finger and the key it controls—to
memorize the new key location.

Step 2—New Key Try-out

Keep elbows close to body.

```
d3d k8k d3d k8k d3d k8k d3d k8k d3d k8k d3d k8k
131 313 311 181 818 381 381 381 183 138 318 813

bid 3 bid 3 bid 3 bid 3 oak 8 oak 8 oak 8 oak 8
bid 3 bid 3 bid 3 bid 3 oak 8 oak 8 oak 8 oak 8
```

5. Self-Testing Work: (30 Minutes) Part 1. Sentence Practice. Copy the
following 12 lines exactly as shown. Single spacing.

If keys lock press Margin Release.
Space once after an abbreviation.

```
d3d k8k d3d k8k d3d k8k d3d k8k 318 813 138 813 381
13 kg lamb roast; 38 kg lamb chops; 8 kg bananas;
31 kg lamb chops; 83 kg lamb roast; 3 kg peaches;

lie 3 dye 3 pie 3 dye 3 Fiji 8 Fiji 8 Fiji 8
18 cans grape juice; 138 cans prune juice; 4 kg coffee;
47 cans prune juice; 143 cans grape juice; 8 kg onions;

d3d k8k d3d k8k d3d k8k 183 381 813 318 138 381
8 kg Swiss Cheese; 13 kg Kraft Cheese; 4 kg pears;
5 kg Kraft Cheese; 17 kg Swiss Cheese; 6 kg beans;

pie 3 dye 3 pie 3 dye 3 Fiji 8 Fiji 8 Fiji 8 Fiji
The sum of 13 and 83 and 153 and 75 and 47 is 371
The sum of 47 and 75 and 153 and 83 and 13 is 371
```

Part 2. Paragraph Practice. **Double** spacing. Copy each paragraph **once.**

John Jacob Astor was born in 1763 and died in 1848. He went to America from England in 1784 and set up a prosperous fur trade. In 1811 he founded the settlement of Astoria near the mouth of the Columbia River.

Alexander Graham Bell was born in Scotland on March 3rd, 1847. He invented the telephone in 1876. The Bell Telephone Company was organized in 1877. Mr. Bell also invented the gramophone in 1887.

John Quincy Adams, sixth President of the United States, was born in Massachusetts on July 11th, 1767. In 1817 he was appointed Secretary of State. He died in 1848.

6. Corrective Work: (5 Minutes) As usual.

7. Challenge Work: (5 Minutes) Select any two of the above paragraphs; then challenge yourself to turn out at least one of them **perfectly.**

LESSON 18

Aim: (*a*) To develop sustained typing skill by 5-Minute Timings.

(*b*) To learn to use the figures **2** and **9**.

1. Machine Adjustments: See Lesson 2.

2. Warm-up: (5 Minutes) Copy the first two lines exactly as shown; then throw the carriage twice and type the sentence 10 times.

```
f4f j7j f5f j6j d3d k8k f4f j7j f5f j6j d3d k8k
or4 ru7 it5 by6 ie3 ok8 or4 ru7 it5 by6 ie3 ok8.

The sum of 14 and 16 and 53 and 58 and 174 is 315.
```

3. Skill-Building Work: (20 Minutes)

(*a*) Preview Practice on Words and Phrases .... 3 minutes

(*b*) Two 1-Minute Timings and Word Practice .... 3 minutes

(*c*) Two 5-Minute Timings and Word Practice ....14 minutes

—

20 minutes

First: **Preview Practice.** Practise each of the following words and phrases 3 times:

```
strike...centre...finger...spring...though...
expert...sharply...release...quickly...develop...
letting...squarely...practice...familiar...
fingertip...important...technique...releasing...
instantly...it is...do it...do this...with the...
you get.
```

Second: **Machine Adjustments.**

(*a*) Remove all tab stops.

(*b*) Set a Tab Stop 5 spaces from left margin.

(*c*) Set Line Space Gauge for **double** spacing.

Third: **Two 1-Minute Timings.**

Take two 1-Minute Timings on the following paragraph.

65

Repeat the copy if you finish before end of minute. This is a Warm-up for the 5-Minute Timing.

```
                          5
    Strike eaoh key sharply with the fingertip and
  10                              15
squarely in the centre.  Strike the key quickly,
    20                            25
letting the finger spring back as though the key
      30   31
were red hot.
```

Fourth: **Two 5-Minute Timings.** Relax a while; then take two 5-Minute Timings on the copy following. Repeat if you finish before end of 5 minutes. Try to maintain your best 1-minute rate.

```
                          5
    Strike each key sharply with the fingertip and
  10                              15
squarely in the centre.  Strike the key quickly,
    20                            25
letting the finger spring back as though the key
      30
were red hot.
                    35                          40
    To type fast, it is just as important to release
                    45                          50
the key quickly as it is to strike it quickly.  Expert
                55                      60
typists do this; you too, can do it, with practice.
                65                          70
    One good way to develop this technique is to
                75                          80
practise familiar words and phrases.  Type them over
                85                      90
and over again until you get the knack of hitting the
                95                      100  101
keys quickly and releasing the fingers instantly.
```

REMINDER: (*a*) See in which 5-Minute Timing you typed the most correct words per minute. That is your best score. Enter it in your Personal Progress Record—the 5-Minute Timed Typing Score Sheet which you established in Lesson 15.

(*b*) Practise the words in which you made
errors—after each timing.

4. New Key Control: (10 Minutes) Learning to use figures **2** and **9**.
Figure **2** is controlled by the **S** finger.
Figure **9** is controlled by the **L** finger.

Step 1—New Key Preview

Reach and feel the centre of each new key—with the fingertip: then
return the finger quickly to its home base. Repeat this fingering
several times. Think of the finger and the key it controls—to memorize the new key location.

Step 2—New Key Try-out

Keep elbows close to body.

```
s2s s2s s2s s2s s2s s2s 191 191 191 191 191 191
s2s 191 s2s 191 s2s 191 s2s 191 s2s 191 s2s 191

bow 2 bow 2 bow 2 bow 2 two 9 two 9 two 9 two 9
bow 2 two 9 bow 2 two 9 bow 2 two 9 bow 2 two 9
```

5. Self-Testing Work: (30 Minutes) Part 1. Sentence Practice. Copy the
following 12 lines exactly as shown. Single spacing.

If keys lock, press Margin Release.

```
s2s 191 s2s 191 s2s 191 s2s 191 s2s 191 s2s 191 s2s 191
12 kg coffee; 19 kg Cottage Cheese; 9 kg peaches;
19 kg apples; 29 kg Cheddar Cheese; 2 kg banana;

low 2 fro 9 low 2 fro 9 low 2 fro 9 low 2 fro 9 29 192;
9 kg Smoked Tongue; 2 kg tomatoes; 9 kg avocados;
2 kg Cooked Tongue; 9 kg avocados; 2 kg tomatoes;

s2s 191 s2s 191 219 921 192 s2s 191 s2s 191 291 129
The sum of 29 and 86 and 33 and 92 and 52 is 292.
The sum of 52 and 92 and 86 and 33 and 29 is 292.

ow 2 to 9 ow 2 to 9 we 23 ok 98 we 23 ok 98 s2s 191
George Washington was born on February 22nd, 1732.
Horatio Alger was born in 1834 and died in 1899.
```

Part 2. Paragraph Practice. **Double** spacing. Copy each paragraph **once.**
Space once after initials.

Christopher Latham Sholes was the inventor of the
first practical typewriter. He was born in Columbia
County, Pennsylvania, February 14th, 1819.

James Monroe, fifth President of The United States,
was born on April 28th, 1758. In 1782 he entered politics.
In 1799 he was appointed Governor of Virginia. In 1811
he became Secretary of State; in 1814, Secretary of War;
in 1816, President of The United States.

On September 1st, 1939, Germany launched undeclared
war on Poland. On September 3rd, 1939, Great Britain
declared war on Germany. On December 8th, 1941, The
United States declared war against the Axis.

Samuel F. B. Morse, inventor and artist, was born
in 1791 and died in 1872. In 1829 he went to Europe
for three years. For 12 years he worked on perfecting
the electrical telegraph, which was exhibited at New
York University in 1837.

6. Corrective Work: (5 Minutes) As usual.

7. Challenge Work: (5 Minutes) Try another copy of the above second
paragraph. Challenge yourself to a **perfect** job.

LESSON 19

Aim: (*a*) To develop sustained typing skill by 5-Minute Timings.

(*b*) To learn to use the Figure **0** and the **-** (Hyphen).

1. Machine Adjustments: See Lesson 2.

2. Warm-up: (5 Minutes) Copy the first two lines exactly as shown; then throw the carriage twice and type the sentence 10 times.

```
f4f  j7j  f5f  j6j  d3d  k8k  s2s  191  f4f  j7j  f5f  j6j
s2s  191  d3d  k8k  f4f  j7j  f5f  j6j  f4f  j7j  f5f  j6j
```

```
The sum of 47 and 65 and 38 and 92 and 16 equals 258.
```

3. Skill-Building Work: (20 Minutes)

(*a*) Preview Practice on Words and Phrases .... 3 minutes

(*b*) Two 1-Minute Timings and Word Practice .... 3 minutes

(*c*) Two 5-Minute Timings and Word Practice ....14 minutes

—

20 minutes

First: **Preview Practice.** Each word and phrase 3 times:

```
expert...typing...margin...always...before...
permits...others...reached...equipped...machines...
carriage...typewriter...approaching...you are...
of the...for the...on the...you may...before the
```

Second: **Machine Adjustments for Timed Typing.**

(*a*) Remove all tab stops.

(*b*) Set a Tab Stop 5 spaces from left margin.

(*c*) Set Line Space Gauge for **double** spacing.

Third: **Two 1-Minute Timings.**

```
                        5
     Your typewriter is equipped with a bell which
      10                      15
rings to warn you that you are approaching the end
      20   21
of the line.
```

REMINDER: Score the better of the two 1-Minute Timings. Try to maintain that rate on the 5-Minute Timings.

Fourth: **Two 5-Minute Timings.**

```
                         5
     Your typewriter is equipped with a bell which
     10                         15
rings to warn you that you are approaching the end
     20
of the line.
                    25                        30
     On some machines, the bell rings five spaces
                         35                        40
before the margin stop is reached; on other machines,
                         45                        50
it rings when there are six or seven spaces left.
                    55
     The ring of the bell permits you to keep your
 60                            65
eyes on the copy.  When you hear the bell, finish
  70                           75
the word you are typing and throw the carriage for
  80
the next line.
                    85                             90
     Do not look up to watch for the end of the line;
                    95                        100
you may lose your place in the copy.  Always keep
               105                        110
your eyes on the copy like the expert typist.
```

REMINDER: (*a*) Score the better of the two 5-Minute timings.

(*b*) Enter the result in your Personal Progress Record.

4. New Key Control (10 Minutes) Learning to use Figure **0** and - (Hyphen).

0 is controlled by the **L** finger. Use left shift key.

- is controlled by the **semicolon** finger.

Step 1—New Key Preview

Reach and touch the centre of each new key—with the fingertip; then
return the finger quickly to its home base. Repeat this fingering
several times. Think of the finger and the key it controls—to memorize new key location.

Step 2—New Key Try-out

```
;p-; ;p-; ;p-; ;p-; ;p-; ;p-; ;p-; ;p-; ;p-; ;p-; ;p-;
;-p; ;-p; ;-p; ;-p; ;-p; ;-p; ;-p; ;-p; ;-p; ;-p; ;-p;

10-room; 10-room; 10-room; 10-room; 10-room;
20-room; 20-room; 20-room; 20-room; 20-room;
```

5. Self-Testing Work: (30 Minutes) Part 1. Sentence Practice. Copy the
following 12 lines exactly as shown. Single spacing.

> *Space once after semicolon.*
> *Space twice after colon.*
> *Strike hyphen with space either side for dash.*

```
f4f j7j f5f j6j d3d k8k s2s 191 ;0; ;-; ;0; ;-;
one-half; one-fourth; one-eighth; three-quarters;
one-half; two-thirds; one-fourth; three-sevenths;

f4f j7j f5f j6j d3d k8k s2s 191 ;0; ;-; ;0; ;-;
20-room house; 30-room house; 40-room house;
50-room house; 60-room house; 70-room house;

f4f j7j f5f j6j d3d k8k s2s 191 ;0; ;-; ;0; ;-;
one-half; one-fourth; one-eighth; three-quarters;
one-half; two-thirds; one-fourth; three-sevenths;

f4f j7j f5f j6j d3d k8k s2s 191 ;0; ;-; ;0; ;-;
Every expert was once a beginner - with ambition.
Every expert was once a beginner - with ambition.
```

Part 2. Paragraph Practice. **Double** spacing. Copy each paragraph **once.**

> *Do not space before or after the hyphen.*
> *Do not space before or after the comma in figures.*

```
As you have seen in the above sentence practice,
```

the hyphen is used for typing compound words. Here
are a few more examples: up-to-date, first-class,
by-product.

The hyphen is used also to divide words between
syllables at the end of the line. When the bell rings,
finish the word if it is short - less than six letters.
If the word is longer, divide it at the end of a
syllable.

The hyphens in the following words show where
they could be divided at the end of a line: after-
noon, state-ment, hesi-tate, cer-ti-fi-cate, exami-
na-tion.

The sum of 10 and 20 and 30 and 40 and 50 and
60 and 70 and 80 and 90 and 100 and 105 and 106 and
107 and 108 and 109 and 110 equals 1,195.

6. Corrective Work: (5 Minutes) As usual.

7. Challenge Work: (5 Minutes) Here is a new paragraph. Challenge
yourself to turn out a **perfect** copy—on the first trial:
> *Do not space after the first initial in a.m. and p.m.*

Have you see the new 7-room house at 175 West
Street? It is equipped with every up-to-date,
labour-saving device for the home. You may inspect
it free of charge any day except Sunday between
10 a.m. and 4 p.m.

LESSON 20

Aim: (*a*) To develop sustained typing skill by 5-Minute Timings.

(*b*) To learn **Horizontal Centring** (Equal Left and Right Margins).

1. Machine Adjustments: See Lesson 2.

2. Warm-up: (5 Minutes) Copy the first two lines exactly as shown; then throw the carriage twice and type the sentence 10 times.

```
f4f j7j f5f j6j d3d k8k s2s 191 ;0; f4f j7j f5f
;q; ;½; ;-; ;q; ;½; ;-; ;q; ;½; ;-; ;q; ;½; ;-;

The basic per hour rate of 50p was raised to 75p.
```

3. Skill-Building Work: (20 Minutes)

(*a*) Preview Practice on Words and Phrases .... 3 minutes

(*b*) Two 1-Minute Timings and Word Practice .... 3 minutes

(*c*) Two 5-Minute Timings and Word Practice ....14 minutes

20 minutes

First: **Preview Practice.** Each word and phrase 3 times.

```
useful...number...devices...example...machine...
carriage...printing...midpoint...backspace...
whichever...indicator...typewriter...impression...
centring...time-saving...of the...at the...in the...
if you...you have...from the...on your
```

Second: **Machine Adjustments for Timed Typing.**

(*a*) Remove tab stops.

(*b*) Set a Tab Stop 5 spaces from left margin.

(*c*) Set Line Space Gauge for **double** spacing.

Third: **Two 1-Minute Timings.**

```
                  5
The backspace key is one of the most useful
   10                    15
time-saving devices on your typewriter.  You use
```

73

```
        20                        25
it to back up a space, or to darken a light
            29
impression.
```

REMINDER: (*a*) Score the better of the two 1-Minute Timings.

(*b*) Try to maintain that rate on the 5-Minute Timings.

Fourth: **Two 5-Minute Timings.**

```
                        5
      The backspace key is one of the most useful time-
10                        15                        20
saving devices on your typewriter.  You use it to back
                        25                        30
up a space, to darken a light impression, or to pivot.
            35                        40
To pivot means to type a line so that the last letter
            45                        50
is at the right margin or other chosen point.
                        55                        60
      For example, if you want a date line to end at
                        65                        70
the right margin, place the carriage with the printing
                75                        80
point indicator at the right margin and backspace once
            85
for each stroke in the date line.
            90                                95
      The most important use of the backspace key is in
            100                103
centring words or lines.
```

REMINDER: (*a*) Score the better of the two 5-Minute Timings.

(*b*) Enter the result in your Personal Progress Record.

4. New Work: (15 Minutes) Learning Horizontal Centring.

Horizontal centring means typing material across the paper so that the left and right margins are equal.

To centre horizontally: (*a*) Set the carriage at the centre—40 for Pica type; 48 for Elite type.

(*b*) Backspace once for each two strokes in the material to be centred. If one letter is left over, ignore it.

Fig. 16. Location of Backspace Key. Some Typewriters show an Arrow.

New Work:

A. To centre the word INDEPENDENCE
   1. Set carriage at centre (40 or 48).
   2. Backspace **once** for each two strokes as you say,
      IN DE PE ND EN CE
   3. Type the word.

B. To centre the word EDUCATION
   1. Set carriage at centre (40 or 48).
   2. Backspace **once** for each two strokes as you say, ED UC AT IO (Disregard N).
   3. Type the word.

C. To centre the name SINCLAIR B. REMINGTON
   1. Set carriage at centre (40 or 48).
   2. Backspace **once** for each two strokes as you say, SI NC LA IR Space B Full stop Space RE MI NG TO (Disregard N).
   3. Type the name.

5. Self-Testing Work: (30 Minutes) Now test your knowledge of horizontal centring. Centre each of the following lines. Single space. Throw carriage twice after each group.

```
George Washington              THE POWER OF POSITIVE THINKING
Sir Winston Churchill          FOR YOUNG PEOPLE
James Madison                  by
Andrew Jackson                 Norman Vincent Peale

Dr. Albert Schweitzer          You are Invited
Medical Missionary             to attend
Philosopher                    The 1956 BUSINESS SHOW
Man of God                     Grand Central Palace
                               January 19th to 25th
                               7 to 9 p.m.
```

6. Challenge Work: (5 Minutes) Try for a **perfect** centring job of these two advertisements:

```
                    THE GENERAL MOTORS SHOW
                    Waldorf-Astoria
                    Week of January 16th
                    Admission Free
                    Bring a Friend

                    DINE OUT TONIGHT
                    at one of these
                    BETTER PLACES
                    China Bowl
                    Little Vienna
                    Little Hungary
```

LESSON 21

Aim: (*a*) To develop sustained typing skill by 5-Minute Timings.

(*b*) To learn **Vertical Centring** (Equal Top and Bottom Margins).

1. Machine Adjustments: See Lesson 2.

2. Warm-up: (5 Minutes) Copy the first line exactly as shown; then throw the carriage twice and type the sentence 10 times.

```
f4f j7j f5f j6j d3d k8k s2s 191 ;0; ;-; 191 ;0; ;-;

Send at once 165 pads, 370 books, and 248 pencils.
```

3. Skill-Building Work: (20 Minutes)

(*a*) Preview Practice on Words and Phrases .... 3 minutes

(*b*) Two 1-Minute Timings and Word Practice .... 3 minutes

(*c*) Two 5-Minute Timings and Word Practice ....14 minutes

20 minutes

First: **Preview Practice.** Each word and phrase 3 times.

```
equal...bottom...number...eleven...vertical...
subtract...centring...sixty-six...available...
remainder...it is...in the...of your...so that...
from the
```

Second: **Machine Adjustments for Timed Typing.**

(*a*) Remove all tab stops.

(*b*) Set a Tab Stop 5 spaces from left margin.

(*c*) Set Line Space Gauge for **double** spacing.

Third: **Two 1-Minute Timings.**

```
                          5
    Vertical centring means typing material on a
         10                    15
page so that the top and bottom margins are about
         20
equal.
```

77

Fourth: **Two 5-Minute Timings.**

                              5
    Vertical centring means typing material on a
    10   15
page so that the top and bottom margins are about
        20
equal.
                                  25
    First, measure the length of your paper. If
    30   35
you are using A4 typing paper, it is 11.69 inches long
            40   45
(297 mm). You can type six lines to the vertical
            50   55
inch; so your paper allows you to type seventy
                60
lines from top to bottom.
                        65   70
    To centre vertically, count the lines and spaces
                        75   80
in the material to be centred. Subtract that number
                85
from seventy, which is the total number of lines
    90
available on the paper.
        95   100
    Divide the remainder by two, to get the number
        105   110
of lines from the top edge on which the typing should
    114
start.

4. New Work: (15 minutes) Learning Vertical Centring. Vertical centring means typing material on a page so that the top and bottom margins are about equal.

To centre material vertically (from top to bottom):

    (*a*) Count the typewritten lines and blank lines in the material to be centred. Jot down the total.

    (*b*) Subtract the total from 70, which is the number of typing lines on a full sheet of A4 typing paper. For a half sheet, subtract from 35. The remainder is the number of single spaces left for top and bottom margins.

(c) Divide the remainder by 2. This gives you the number of spaces from the top edge for your starting point. Disregard fractions.

EXAMPLE: To centre 25 lines (typewritten and blank) on a
full sheet, subtract 25 from 70 70
Lines Required .... −25

Lines left for top and bottom margins 45
Divide 45 in half: $45 \div 2 = 22\frac{1}{2}$
Start typing on line 23 from top edge of paper.

New Work: Centre the following advertisement on a full sheet:

ACME MARKET
Money-Saving Buys

BEEF ROLLED RIB
30p kg

FRANKFURTERS
20p kg

SMOKED TONGUE
35p kg

SIRLOIN STEAK
50p kg

Follow these steps:

1. Count the typewritten lines (10)
2. Count the blank lines between the typewritten lines (4)
3. Add the typewritten lines and the blank lines (14)
4. Subtract 14 lines from the total number of lines which the paper accommodates: 70 minus 14 equals 56
5. Divide 56 by 2; Result: 28
6. Single space 28 times from top edge of the paper
7. Set the carriage at the centre—40 for Pica; 48 for Elite
8. Centre the first line ACME MARKET
9. Single space and centre: Money-Saving Buys
10. Double space and centre: BEEF ROLLED RIB

NOTE: Follow the above steps until you have centred the last line: 50p kg.

5. Self-Testing Work: (30 Minutes) Centre horizontally and vertically each of the following 2 advertisements on an A4 sheet.

REMINDER: (*a*) You can type 6 lines to the vertical inch (25.4 mm).

(*b*) A4 typing paper is 11.69 inches long (297 mm); so it allows you to type 70 lines from top to bottom.

(1) FOOTBALL GAME

    High School of Commerce
    Vs.
    De Witt Clinton High School

    May 18th,
    at
    EBBETTS FIELD

    Game Starts at 2.30
    Bring a Friend

(2) EXCITING TOURS

    To

    THE ORIENT
    and
    THE THOUSAND ISLANDS
    Arranged by
    WONDER-TOURS COMPANY
    615 Caversham Avenue,
    London, W.1.

Centre No. 3 and No. 4, each on a half sheet.

REMINDER: (*a*) A half sheet allows you to type 35 lines.

(*b*) Subtract the total number of typewritten and blank lines from 35 then divide by 2— to give you the number of spaces from the top edge for your starting point.

(3) THIS BOOK

    is
    from

    THE LIBRARY

    of

    JAMES MONROE HIGH SCHOOL
    Birmingham

(4) MOTOR BOAT SHOW

    Now At

    KINGSBRIDGE ARMOURY

    January 15th-23rd

    Admission 10p

    3 p.m. to 9.30 p.m.

6. Challenge Work: (5 Minutes) Try for a **perfect** centring job of the following advertisement on a full sheet:

ADULT EDUCATION
Hunter College
School of Education
Park Avenue

EVENING COURSES
for

Men and Women
15-Week Term
Beginning
February 10th
REGISTER NOW

LESSON 22

Aim: (*a*) To develop sustained typing skill by 5-Minute Timings.

(*b*) To learn to use the keys: @ (At) and & (Ampersand).

1. Machine Adjustments: See Lesson 2.

2. Warm-up: (5 Minutes) Copy the first line exactly as shown; then throw the carriage twice and type the sentence 10 times.

```
f4f j7j f5f j6j d3d k8k s2s 191 ;0; ;-; 191 ;0; ;-;

The fraction one-half may be typewritten as ½.
```

3. Skill-Building Work: (20 Minutes)

 (*a*) Preview Practice on Words and Phrases .... 3 minutes

 (*b*) Two 1-Minute Timings and Word Practice .... 3 minutes

 (*c*) Two 5-Minute Timings and Word Practice ....14 minutes

               ―

               20 minutes

First: **Preview Practice.** Each word and phrase 3 times:

```
cannot...margin...typing...device...enough...
before...spaces...enables...located...releases...
machines...typewriter...at the...you are...on the...
and the...it is...you have...on which
```

Second: **Machine Adjustments for Timed Typing.**

 (*a*) Clear all tab stops.

 (*b*) Set a Tab Stop 5 spaces from left margin.

 (*c*) Set Line Space Gauge for **double** spacing.

Third: **Two 1-Minute Timings.**

```
                      5
     Your typewriter has a key that releases the
     10                        15
margin lock and enables you to finish a word at the
     20    21
end of a line.
```

Fourth: **Two 5-Minute Timings.**

```
                          5
     Your typewriter has a key that releases the
        10                     15
margin lock and enables you to finish a word at the
        20
end of a line.
                     25                    30
     If you are typing a long word that cannot be
                35                    40
divided and the margin locks before you complete the
                45                    50
word, depress the margin release key.  This will en-
                55
able you to finish the word.
                     60                    65
     On some machines, the margin release key is
                70                    75
located on the right side; on other machines, it is
                80
located on the left side.
                     85
     When the typewriter bell rings, it means that
  90                     95                      100
you have about seven spaces left before the keys lock.
                105                    110
In most cases, when the bell rings, you will have
                115       117
enough spaces left to finish the word.
```

4. New Key Control: (10 Minutes) Learning to use @ and &
@ is controlled by the **F** finger. Use right shift key.
& is controlled by the **J** finger. Use left shift key.

Step 1—New Key Preview

Using the shift key, reach and touch the centre of each new key; then return fingers quickly to home base. Practise it this way—Shift, Reach, Return . . . until you can do it smoothly. Think of the finger and the new key it controls.

Step 2—New Key Try-out

```
f@f  f@f  f@f  f@f  f@f  f@f  f@f  f@f  f@f  f@f  f@f  f@f  f@f
f&j  f&j  f&j  f&j  f&j  f&j  f&j  f&j  f&j  f&j  f&j  f&j  f&j
```

5. Self-Testing Work: (30 Minutes) Part 1. Sentence Practice. Copy the following 9 lines exactly as shown. Single spacing.

Space once after an abbreviation.

```
f@f j&j f@f j&j f@f j&j f@f j&j f@f j&j f@f j&j f@f j&j
Tickets, 25p each; Tickets, 25p each; Tickets, 25p each.
Zuckor & Company; Zuckor & Company; Zuckor & Company;

f@f j&j f@f j&j f@f j&j f@f j&j f@f j&j f@f j&j f@f j&j
Mintz & Co. offer 1952 Cadillac cars.
Dixon & Co. offer 1953 Chrysler cars.

f@f j&j f@f j&j f@f j&j f@f j&j f@f j&j f@f j&j f@f j&j
Fly to Miami non-stop in 3 hrs. 45 mins.
Fly to Tampa non-stop in 3 hrs. 10 mins.
```

Part 2. Paragraph Practice **Double** spacing. Copy each paragraph **once**.

```
    Crane & Co. are going out of business on May 28th.
To clear out their entire stock, they offer cotton
skirts, formerly sold at 87p, at the money-saving
price of 50p.
    De Voux & Co., fashion designers, offer coats
at money-saving prices. They also offer cocktail
gowns, slightly soiled, at greatly reduced prices.
```

6. Corrective Work: (5 Minutes) As usual.

7. Challenge Work: (5 Minutes) Challenge yourself to turn out a **perfect** copy of the following paragraph:

REMINDER: (*a*) One space either side of the hyphen - for a dash.

(*b*) Space once after the full stop in an abbreviation.

```
Smith & Co. offer foam cushions at 50p - a

saving of 20p. Brooks & Co. offer kitchen chairs

at 95p - a saving of 60p. Wilkins & Co. offer

double-track storm windows and screen at greatly

reduced prices.
```

LESSON 23

Aim: (*a*) To develop sustained typing skill by 5-Minute Timings.

(*b*) To learn to use **£** (Pound) and __ (Underscore) keys.

1. Machine Adjustments: See Lesson 2.

2. Warm-up: (5 Minutes) Copy the first two lines exactly as shown; then throw the carriage twice and type the sentence 10 times.

```
fr4 fr4 fr4 f@f f@f f@f ju7 ju7 ju7 j&j j&j j&j
f@f j&j f@f j&j f@f j&j f@f j&j f@f j&j f@f j&j

Fox & Co., offer Refrigerators at reduced prices.
```

3. Skill-Building Work: (20 Minutes)

(*a*) Preview Practice on Words and Phrases .... 3 minutes

(*b*) Two 1-Minute Timings and Word Practice .... 3 minutes

(*c*) Two 5-Minute Timings and Word Practice ....14 minutes

20 minutes

First: **Preview Practice.** Each word and phrase 3 times.

```
others...typing...awkward...quickly...slowing
possible...increase...practice...smoothly...
familiar...trouble...difficult...particular...
it is...at the...you can...and the...have been
that are...with the...you will...for you
```

Second: **Machine Adjustments for Timed Typing.**

(*a*) Clear all tab stops.

(*b*) Set a Tab Stop 5 spaces from left margin.

(*c*) Set Line Space Gauge for **double** spacing.

Third: **Two 1-Minute Timings.**

```
                       5
     It is not possible to type all words at the same
10                      15                      20
speed.  Some words are easy to type; others are very
                23
awkward to finger.
```

86

Fourth: **Two 5-Minute Timings.**

<pre>
                            5
        It is not possible to type all words at the same
   10   15   20
   speed. Some words are easy to type; others are very

   awkward to finger.
              25   30
        You can increase your typing speed and accuracy
              35   40
   by typing the awkward words slowly and the easy ones
           45   50
   quickly. Practise the words which give you trouble.
        55   60
   Practise both the easy and difficult words until you
        65   70
   can type them smoothly and accurately.
                     75   80
        After a while, you will be familiar with the
                     85   90
   words that have been slowing you down, and at the
                     95   100
   same time you will know which words you can type
                        105   110
   fast. Soon you will type all the words more smoothly
                  113
   and accurately.
</pre>

4. New Key Control: (10 Minutes) Learning to use £ and __ (Under-score).

£ is controlled by the **F** finger. Use right shift key.
__ is controlled by the **J** finger. Use left shift key.

Step 1—New Key Preview

Using the shift key, reach and touch the centre of each new key; then return fingers quickly to home base. Practise it this way—Shift, Reach, Return . . . until you can do it smoothly. Think of the finger and the new key it controls.

Step 2—New Key Try-out

To underscore, first type the word; then backspace to the first letter, and strike the underscore for each letter.

```
f£f f£f f£f f£f f£f f£f j_j j_j j_j j_j j_j j_j
Deduct £5. Deduct £5. Deduct £5. Deduct £5.
Do it now. Do it now. Do it now. Do it now.
```

5. **Self-Testing Work:** (30 Minutes) Part 1. Sentence Practice. Copy the following 6 lines exactly as shown. Single spacing. Throw carriage twice after every third line.

TYPING TIP: *To underscore one word, use the shift key. To underscore a series of words, use the* **shift lock**. *Strike the underscore as you spell each word letter by letter.*

```
f£f j_j f£f j_j f£f j_j f£f j_j f£f j_j f£f j_j f£f
Prompt service; Lowest prices; Expert workmanship;
Underscore for emphasis. Underscore for emphasis.

f£f j_j f£f j_j f£f j_j f£f j_j f£f j_j f£f j_j f£f j_j
Save from £2 to £5 on superb quality jackets.
Save from £1 to £2 on superb quality blouses.
```

> *In figures, do not space before or after the comma.*
> *Do not space before or after the decimal point.*

Part 2. Paragraph Practice. **Double** spacing. Copy each paragraph **once**.

```
    Messrs. Cox & Vinson are not entitled to the
discount of £4 which they have deducted from our invoice
of November 27th.

    James inherited £1,500 from his father.  This
sum he invested in industrial shares which yield him
an income of £100 per annum.

    You may deduct a discount of £3 from the prices
quoted for our refrigerators shown on page 75 of our
catalogue.  If payment is made within 10 days after
the date of the invoice, you may deduct an extra £1
discount.
```

6. Corrective Work: (5 Minutes) As usual.

7. Challenge Work: (5 Minutes) Here is another challenge to your ability to type a **perfect** paragraph:

Messrs. Lenox & Smith advertise Oriental rugs in the following quantities and sizes: 50 Lillehans, size 9 x 15 at £290; 25 Persian Sarouks, size 8 x 12 at £275; 18 Kutajah rugs, size 12 x 14 at £260. All sales for cash only.

LESSON 24

Aim: (*a*) To develop sustained typing skill by 5-Minute Timings.
    (*b*) To learn to use **/** (Slant) and **'** (Apostrophe).

1. Machine Adjustments: See Lesson 2.

2. Warm-up: (5 Minutes) Copy the first two lines exactly as shown; then throw the carriage twice and type the sentence 10 times.

```
frf f4f juj j7j j&j ftf f5f jyj j6j j_j frf f4f
frf f4f juj j7j j&j ftf f5f jyj j6j j_j frf f4f


Zale & De Veaux offer Blue Serge at £5 a piece.
```

3. Skill-Building Work: (20 Minutes)

    (*a*) Preview Practice on Words and Phrases .... 3 minutes
    (*b*) Two 1-Minute Timings and Word Practice .... 3 minutes
    (*c*) Two 5-Minute Timings and Word Practice ....14 minutes
                                              —
                                              20 minutes

First: **Preview Practice.** Each word and phrase 3 times.

```
strike...lightly...learned...general...material
centred...necessary...centring...difficult...
sometimes...backspacer...appearance...attractive
impressions...horizontally...in the...to be...
with the...will be...has been
```

Second: **Machine Adjustments for Timed Typing.**

    (*a*) Clear all tab stops.
    (*b*) Set a Tab Stop 5 spaces from left margin.
    (*c*) Set Line Space Gauge for **double** spacing.

Third: **Two 1-Minute Timings.**

```
                          5
     To avoid light and dark impressions on the page,
10                       15                          20
strike every key with the same force.  If you strike
```

25   30
every key with the same force, every letter will be
                        34
of the same shade.

Fourth: **Two 5-Minute Timings.**

                              5
     To avoid light and dark impressions on the page,
  10   15   20
strike every key with the same force. If you strike
                        25   30
every key with the same force, every letter will be
                        35   40
of the same shade and the general appearance of your
                        45
work will be attractive.

                              50
     Sometimes, of course, it may be necessary to
  55   60
darken a letter that has been struck very lightly
     65   70
and is difficult to read. In such case, use the
       75   80
backspacer and strike the letter again lightly.
            85   90
     The backspacer is used also for centring
                        95   100
horizontally. As you have learned, you set the
                       105   110
carriage at the centre of the page and backspace
                       115
once for every two strokes in the material to be
  120   121
centred.

4. New Key Control: (10 Minutes) Learning to use **/** and **'** keys.
          / is controlled by the **D** finger. Use right shift key.
          ' is controlled by the **K** finger. Use left shift key.

Step 1—New Key Preview

Using the shift key, reach and touch the centre of each new key; then
return fingers quickly to home base. Follow these steps—Shift,
Reach, Return . . . until you can do it smoothly. Think of the finger
and the key it controls.

Step 2—New Key Try-out

```
d/d d/d d/d d/d d/d d/d k'k k'k k'k k'k k'k k'k
d/d k'k d/d k'k d/d k'k d/d k'k d/d k'k d/d k'k
8 o'clock; 8 o'clock; 8 o'clock; 8 o'clock; 8 o'clock;
```

5. **Self-Testing Work:** (30 Minutes) Part 1. Sentence Practice. Copy the
following 6 lines exactly as shown. Single spacing.
For exclamation mark: type full stop, backspace, and type apostrophe.
(Some typewriters have a ready-made exclamation mark which should,
of course, be used for working purposes.)

```
d/d k'k d/d k'k d/d k'k d/d k'k d/d k'k d/d k'k
d/d k'k d/d k'k d/d k'k d/d k'k d/d k'k d/d k'k

d/d k'k d/d k'k d/d k'k d/d k'k d/d k'k d/d k'k
The dockers arrived at the docks at 8 o'clock.

d/d k'k d/d k'k d/d k'k d/d k'k d/d k'k d/d k'k
He left the yard at 7 o'clock this morning.
```

Part 2. Paragraph Practice. **Double** spacing. Copy each paragraph **once.**

```
    To make an exclamation mark, type an apostrophe,

backspace, and type a full stop lightly.  Space twice

after an exclamation mark at the end of a sentence,

as you do after a full stop and after a question mark.

    The exclamation mark is used after words,

phrases, or sentences to indicate surprise or strong

emotion.  Examples:  it's truly amazing!  It's a lie!

These pens are guaranteed for 10 years!

    Meet me at my office - room 295 - at 9 o'clock,

Thursday, February 27th.  Mr. Zims of Dixson & O'Brien
```

will be there to discuss their contract for construct-

ing the warehouse.

6. Corrective Work: (5 Minutes) As usual.

7. Challenge Work: (5 Minutes) Aim for a **perfect** copy of the following
paragraph—on your first try!

The consignment of glass jars weighing 325 kg

and costing 5p each was forwarded on September 14th.

Another consignment of jars, estimated to weigh 350 kg

and costing 10p each, is now being loaded and should

reach you this week.

LESSON 25

Aim: *(a)* To develop sustained typing skill by 5-Minute Timings.

(*b*) To learn to use the ( ) (Parentheses).

1. Machine Adjustments: See Lesson 2.

2. Warm-up: (5 Minutes) Copy the first two lines exactly as shown; then throw the carriage twice and type the sentence 10 times:

```
f4f f@f j&j j&j f5f f£f j6j j_j d3d d/d k8k k'k
d3d d/d k'k k8k f4f f@f j7j j&j f5f f£f j6j j_j

Cox Service Company's bonds, Serial No. 59, yield £6
per cent.
```

3. Skill-Building Work: (20 Minutes)

(*a*) Preview Practice on Words and Phrases .... 3 minutes

(*b*) Two 1-Minute Timings and Word Practice .... 3 minutes

(*c*) Two 5-Minute Timings and Word Practice ....14 minutes

20 minutes

First: **Preview Practice.** Each word and phrase 3 times:

```
margin...divide...always...experts...warning...
possible...carriage...division...syllable
separate...necessary...pronounced...at the...
to the...for the...you will...do not...from the
```

Second: **Machine Adjustments for Time Typing.**

(*a*) Clear all tab stops.

(*b*) Set a Tab Stop 5 spaces from left margin.

(*c*) Set Line Space Gauge for **double** spacing.

Third: **Two 1-Minute Timings.**

```
                     5
      Try to keep the right margin as even as possible.
10                   15                        20
Experts always do so. Of course, every now and then,
```
94

```
              25                    30
it is necessary to divide a word at the end of a line,
          35        37
but you should avoid doing so.
```

Fourth: **Two 5-Minute Timings.**

```
                       5
     Try to keep the right margin as even as possible.
10                     15                          20
Experts always do so.  Of course, every now and then,
              25                          30
it is necessary to divide a word at the end of a line,
              35
but you should avoid doing so.
              40                          45
     Listen for the warning bell.  When it rings,
                   50                     55
finish the word and throw the carriage for the next
              60                          65
line.  Thus, you will not have to divide many words.
                   70                     75
Here are a few simple rules for word division:
                        80
     First, divide only after a full syllable.
    85                          90
Second, do not divide a word that is pronounced as
     95                          100
one syllable, such as: though, shipped, bought.
         105                     110
Third, do not separate one letter from the rest of
     114
a word.
```

4. New Key Control: (10 Minutes) Learning to use ( ) (Parentheses).

Left parenthesis (is controlled by the **L** finger. Use left shift key.

Right parenthesis) is controlled by the **;** finger. Use left shift key.

Step 1—New Key Preview

Using the left shift key, reach and touch the centre of each new key; then return fingers quickly to home base. Finger each new key as you say it to yourself—to memorize its location.

Step 2—New Key Try-out

Keep elbows close to body.

```
1(1 1(1 1(1 1(1 1(1 1(1 ;); ;); ;); ;); ;); ;);
1(1 ;); 1(1 ;); 1(1 ;); 1(1 ;); 1(1 ;); 1(1 ;);
```

5. Self-Testing Work: (30 Minutes) Part 1. Sentence Practice. Copy the following 9 lines exactly as shown. Single spacing.

```
1(1 ;); 1(1 ;); 1(1 ;); 1(1 ;); 1(1 ;); 1(1 ;);
one (1) two (2) three (3) four (4) five (5) six (6)
seventy-five (75) eighty-five (85) ninety-five (95)

d/d k'k d/d k'k d/d k'k d/d k'k d/d k'k d/d k'k d/d k'k
Barton's order (dated November 19th) is completed.
Marvin's order (dated February 26th) is completed.

f@f j&j f@f j&j f@f j&j f@f j&j f@f j&j f@f j&j f@f
The price of THE GLOBE (2nd edition) is £2.
The price of THE WORLD (3rd edition) is £3.
```

Part 2. Paragraph Practice. **Double** spacing. Copy each paragraph **once.**

```
The contract specified (a) 12 boxes to a carton;

(b) cartons fastened by wire bands; (c) each carton

plainly identified.

    The Pierce Car Company (reorganized) is now dis-

playing its new 2-passenger car at nine hundred and

fifty pounds (£950).  It will go 18 kilometres (average)

on two litres of petrol.

    To be placed on the free mailing list, please

(1) use school stationery; (2) indicate the business

courses you are teaching; (3) mail your request to

our nearest office.
```

6. Corrective Work: (5 Minutes) As usual.

7. **Challenge Work:** (5 Minutes) Try for a **perfect** copy of the following
   paragraph—on your first attempt.

```
    We understand that the traditional colours in

your school are royal blue (for the girls) and orange

(for the boys).  We shall be glad to furnish the caps

and gowns (made of Lido cloth) in the colours desired

at £8 per outfit.
```

LESSON 26

Aim: (*a*) To develop sustained typing skill by 5-Minute Timings.

   (*b*) To learn to use " (Quotation Marks) and ¼ (One quarter).

1. Machine Adjustments: See Lesson 2.

2. Warm-up: (5 Minutes) Copy the first line exactly as shown; then throw the carriage twice and type the sentence 10 times.

```
f@f j&j f£f j_j d/d k'k l(l ;); d/d k'k l(l ;);
```

```
The banker's home was sold (at a loss) for £9,000.
```

3. Skill-Building Work: (20 Minutes)

     (*a*) Preview Practice on Words and Phrases .... 3 minutes

     (*b*) Two 1-Minute Timings and Word Practice .... 3 minutes

     (*c*) Two 5-Minute Timings and Word Practice ....14 minutes

                                              20 minutes

   First: **Preview Practice.** Each word and phrase 3 times:

```
barely...faster...machine...posture...forward...
loosely...position...directly...slightly...
touching...parallel...keyboard...important...
of the...at the...in the...to the...to it
```

 Second: **Machine Adjustments for Timed Typing.**

     (*a*) Clear all tab stops.

     (*b*) Set a Tab Stop 5 spaces from left margin.

     (*c*) Set Line Space Gauge for **double** spacing.

  Third: **Two 1-Minute Timings.**

```
                      5
     Your position at the machine is more important
  10                      15
than you think.  Good posture will help you to build
  20                      25
your skill at a faster rate.
```

98

Fourth: **Two 5-Minute Timings.**

                           5
       Your position at the machine is more important
    10   15
than you think.   Good posture will help you to build
    20   25
your skill at a faster rate.
                                30
       Use these simple rules of good posture: sit
    35   40
directly in front of the machine, hips well back in
    45   50
the chair, body erect but leaning slightly forward.
    55   60
Let your arms hang loosely at the sides close to the
65
body.

                           70
       Keep all fingers curved like claws and just
    75   80
barely touching the guide keys.   See to it that your
85   90   95
hands are parallel and sloping in the same direction
                        100   105
as the keyboard.   Hold your wrists low but not touching
                   108
the machine.

4. New Key Control: (10 Minutes) Learning to use ” and $\frac{1}{4}$.
       ” is controlled by the S finger. Use right shift key.
       $\frac{1}{4}$ is controlled by the ; finger. Use left shift key.

Step 1—New Key Preview

Using the shift key, reach and touch the centre of each new key; then
return fingers quickly to home base. Finger each new key several
times as you say it to yourself—to memorize its location.

Step 2—New Key Try-out

s"s s"s s"s s"s s"s s"s s"s ;$\frac{1}{4}$; ;$\frac{1}{4}$; ;$\frac{1}{4}$; ;$\frac{1}{4}$; ;$\frac{1}{4}$; ;$\frac{1}{4}$;
s"s ;$\frac{1}{4}$; s"s ;$\frac{1}{4}$; s"s ;$\frac{1}{4}$; s"s ;$\frac{1}{4}$; s"s ;$\frac{1}{4}$; s"s ;$\frac{1}{4}$; s"s

```
"East";  "East";  "East";  "East";  "East";  "East";
"West";  "West";  "West";  "West";  "West";  "West";
```

5. Self-Testing Work: (30 Minutes) Part 1. Sentence Practice. Copy the following 6 lines exactly as shown. Single spacing.

```
s"s ;¼; s"s ;¼; s"s ;¼; s"s ;¼; s"s ;¼; s"s ;¼;
f@f j&j j_j f@f f£f j&j j_j f@f j&j j_j f@f f£f

19 "Zenith" TV Sets £75.  21 "Zenith" TV Sets £83.
19 "Philco" TV Sets £79.  21 "Philco" TV Sets £87.
The steamship "Parthia" (English) arrived on June 10th.
The steamship "Colombo" (Italian) arrived on July 29th.
```

Part 2. Paragraph Practice. **Double** spacing. Copy each paragraph **once**.

```
In this morning's "Times", Associated Market

advertises 5 tins of peaches (California type) at

10p each.  This is 2p a tin less than the lowest

price ever quoted before on this quality.

    Baxter & Company will conduct their sale of

women's "all wool" blue serge suits at 9 a.m.

Monday, January 19th.  All sizes.  Alterations free!

    To celebrate its 35th anniversary, Vim offers

"Welbilt" Gas Cookers for only £50 and "Maytag"

Automatic Washers for only £100.

    The expression "Don't give up the ship" really

means:  "Don't despair.  You can make good."  Those

who succeed are ordinary people who have a "will to

win".
```

6. Corrective Work: (5 Minutes) As usual.

7. Challenge Work: (5 Minutes) Here's another challenge to you. A **perfect** copy of the following paragraph:

Bridget was applying for the position of maid in

a household where the mistress was very particular.

"Have you any references?" asked the mistress.

"Oh, yes, ma'am, lots of them," replied Bridget.

"Then why didn't you bring them with you?"

"Well," the maid explained, "to tell the truth,

they're like my photographs - none of 'em do me

justice."

LESSON 27

Aim: (*a*) To develop sustained typing skill by 5-Minute Timings.

(*b*) To learn to use the fractions ⅜, ¼, ⅜, ⅝, ⅞, and % (Per cent).

1. Machine Adjustments: See Lesson 2.

2. Warm-up: (5 Minutes) Copy the first two lines exactly as shown; then throw the carriage twice and type the sentence 10 times.

```
j&j j_j k'k l(l ;); s"s l(l ;); j&j j_j k'k l)l
k'k j&j j_j s"s l(l ;); l(l ;); k'k j&j j_j s"s

"Don't give up the ship" means "don't despair".
```

3. Skill-Building Work: (20 Minutes)

(*a*) Preview Practice on Words and Phrases .... 3 minutes

(*b*) Two 1-Minute Timings and Word Practice .... 3 minutes

(*c*) Two 5-Minute Timings and Word Practice ....14 minutes

—

20 minutes

First: **Preview Practice.** Each word and phrase 3 times:

```
thought...through...without...success...However...
getting...usually...decided...hastily...definite...
decision...objective...education...to do...it is...
you are...you would...may be...they are
```

Second: **Machine Adjustments for Timed Typing.**

(*a*) Clear all tab stops.

(*b*) Set a Tab Stop 5 spaces from left margin.

(*c*) Set Line Space Gauge for **double** spacing.

Third: **Two 1-Minute Timings.**

```
                         5
        The secretary acts as a personal representative,
10                       15                       20
responsible for the accurate conveying of information
```

```
                        25
to her employer and the accurate issuing of his
  30                            35
communications and instructions.
```

Fourth: Two 5-Minute Timings.

```
                        5
      The secretary acts as a personal representative,
  10                        15                          20
responsible for the accurate conveying of information
                        25
to her employer and the accurate issuing of his
  30                        35
communications and instructions.  The activities of
40                            45
the secretary may vary greatly from employer to
    50                            55
employer, sometimes involving only intelligent
        60                            65
execution of instructions and in other instances
            70                            75
demanding considerable initiative and judgment.  But
        80                            85
the elements of tact and mediation are always apparent.
    90                            95
This is inevitable in the modern world, where the
      100                            105
relationships between business and public, and between
110                            115                        120
business and business are constantly developing new
                    123
ramifications.
```

4. New Key Control: (10 Minutes) Learning to use the fractions $\frac{3}{4}$, $\frac{1}{8}$, $\frac{3}{8}$, $\frac{5}{8}$, $\frac{7}{8}$, and %.

$\frac{3}{4}$ is controlled by the semicolon finger.

$\frac{1}{8}$ is controlled by the semicolon finger. Use left shift key.

$\frac{3}{8}$ is controlled by the semicolon finger.

$\frac{5}{8}$ is controlled by the semicolon finger. Use left shift key.

$\frac{7}{8}$ is controlled by the semicolon finger.

% is controlled by the semicolon finger. Use left shift key.

Step 1—New Key Preview

Using the left shift key, reach and touch the centre of each new key; then return fingers quickly to home base. Finger each new key several times as you say it to yourself.

Step 2—New Key Try-out

Keep elbows close to body. Strike keys sharply.

;¾; ;¾; ;¾; ;¾; ;¾; ;¾; ;⅛; ;⅛; ;⅛; ;⅛; ;⅛; ;⅛;
;⅜; ;⅜; ;⅜; ;⅜; ;⅜; ;⅜; ;⅝; ;⅝; ;⅝; ;⅝; ;⅝; ;⅝;
;⅞; ;⅞; ;⅞; ;⅞; ;⅞; ;⅞; ;%; ;%; ;%; ;%; ;%; ;%;

5. Self-Testing Work: (30 Minutes) Part 1. Sentence Practice. Copy the following 10 lines exactly as shown. Single spacing.

12 boxes less 7¾% discount; 36 pairs less 7⅛% discount.
70 pairs less 6⅞% discount; 50 boxes less 3⅜% discount.

Use the symbol / for fractions such as 2/3, 3/7, 1/10.
Use the symbol / for fractions such as 5/6, 7/9, 4/5.

Be consistent in typing fractions; as, ½, ¼, 1/2, 1/4.
Be consistent in typing fractions; as, ½, ¼, 1/2, 1/4.

Have you received our order No. 78? It amounts to £175.
Have you received our order No. 91? It amounts to £246.

The symbols % and & are used in orders and invoices.
The symbols " and ' are used in orders and invoices.

Part 2. Paragraph Practice. **Double** spacing. Copy each paragraph **once.**

The only fractions on the standard keyboard are, ½, ¼, ¾, ⅛, ⅜, ⅝, ⅞. To make other fractions, use the slant. Here are a few examples: 3/5, 1/10, 1/20. Such fractions are "made" fractions. Do not space before or after the slant.

When typing whole numbers and "made" fractions,

space once between the whole number and the "made"

fraction, e.g. 3 2/5, 4 1/9. When typing whole

numbers with fractions that appear on the keyboard,

do not space after the whole number. Type the whole

number and the fraction as shown in the following

examples:

   Government Bonds yield from $2\frac{1}{2}$% to $3\frac{1}{4}$% interest.

   The distance to the lake was exactly $3\frac{3}{4}$ kilometres.

6. Corrective Work: (5 Minutes) As usual.

7. Challenge Work: (5 Minutes) Try for a **perfect** copy of the following paragraph:

   Find the cost of the following:
       156 kg Butter @ 8p per kg.
       145 Eggs @ 2p each.
       125 tins Soup @ 4p a tin.
       165 kg Sugar @ 4p per kg.

LESSON 28

Aim: *(a)* To develop sustained typing skill by 5-Minute Timings.

(b) To learn to type **Personal Letters—Block Form**.

1. Machine Adjustments: See Lesson 2.

2. Warm-up: (5 Minutes) Copy the first two lines exactly as shown; then throw the carriage twice and type the sentence 10 times.

```
f@f j&j f£f j_j d/d k'k s"s l(l ;); s"s ;);
f@f j&j f£f j_j d/d k'k s"s l(l ;); s"s ;);

See our No. 3 catalogue for boys' "Glider" skates.
```

3. Skill-Building Work: (20 Minutes)

    (a) Preview Practice on Words and Phrases .... 3 minutes

    (b) Two 1-Minute Timings and Word Practice .... 3 minutes

    (c) Two 5-Minute Timings and Word Practice ....14 minutes

                                              —

                                              20 minutes

First: Preview Practice. Each word and phrase 3 times:

```
letter...simpler...picture...personal...business...
otherwise...important...carefully...difference...
attractive...impression...accurately...on the...
for you...you can...to make...there is
```

Second: Machine Adjustments for Timed Typing.

    (a) Clear all tab stops.

    (b) Set a Tab Stop 5 spaces from left margin.

    (c) Set Line Space Gauge for **double** spacing.

Third: Two 1-Minute Timings.

5

```
Letters are of two types - personal and business.
```

```
10                        15                               20
Personal letters are simpler than business letters,
                          25              28
but otherwise, there is little difference.
```

Fourth: **Two 5-Minute Timings.**

```
                            5
     Letters are of two types - personal and business.
10                        15                               20
Personal letters are simpler than business letters,
                          25
but otherwise, there is little difference.
              30                      35
     Every letter you type should look attractive.
              40                      45
The way your letter looks is as important as what
              50                      55
it says.  Your letter speaks for you; so it should,
              60                      65
first of all, make a good impression.
                          70
     Try to keep your right margin as even as you
     75                      80
can.  That makes your letter look neat and carefully
     85                      90
done.  Type accurately.  Centre your letter on the
     95                      100                   104
paper so that it looks like a picture in a frame.
```

4. New Work: (15 Minutes) Typing a Personal Letter—Block Form.

   (*a*) Clear tab stop set for the 5-Minute Timing.

   (*b*) Set a new Tab Stop at the centre—40 (Pica); 48 (Elite).

   (*c*) Set Line Space Gauge for **single** spacing. Margin Stops as before.

   (*d*) Insert an A4 sheet; space up 21 times from top edge. (Vary this according to size of paper and length of letter.)

   (*e*) Type address, date, and closing at the centre. Jump the carriage to that point—press the tab bar or tab key.

   (*f*) Type the date two lines below the address, and the greeting— Dear Tom—four lines below the date.

750 Western Road,
GLOUCESTER
GL2 7YZ.

22nd January, 19...

Address on
line 21
from
top edge.
Start at
centre.

On
line 4
below
date.

Dear Tom,

You can learn touch typing - by yourself.

TYPING MADE SIMPLE - the latest book for
beginners - shows you how. This book
tells you in simple, man-to-man talk,
exactly what to do, how to do it, and how
to keep score of your progress.

Space
twice
between
paragraphs

I've just finished the whole course - 34
lessons. And I'm convinced that touch
typing is easier than you think.

What do you think of this letter - by a
beginner? My average speed is 18 words
a minute. If I can put in about an hour
of practice every day, I think I can soon
boost it to 30.

Let me know how you're doing in your new
job.

Sincerely yours,

Closing
at centre.

┌───┐
│ PERSONAL LETTER—BLOCK FORM   │
└───┘

5. Self-Testing Work: (30 Minutes) Retype the letter to Tom. This time
aim for a **perfect** copy. Then insert a fresh sheet and type the letter
below—to test your skill.

REMINDER: Address on line 21 from top edge—at centre.
Greeting—Dear Alice—on line 4 below date.
Space twice between paragraphs.
Closing—Sincerely— at centre.

```
                    149 Garfield Lane,
                    BANGOR,
                    North Wales.

                    17th June, 19...


Dear Alice,

We were thrilled to hear that you won a
prize in the school essay contest.

Congratulations on your success!  We hope
that you will have many more such happy
accomplishments.

It's quite a while since you last visited
us, and we're so eager to have you with
us again for a few days.  You would never
recognize our bungalow.  Dad and Gerald
have built an extension to the porch and
have repainted the whole place.

Please let me know if you can spend the
first week in July with us so that we
can plan some fun together.

                    Sincerely,
```

6. Number Review: (5 Minutes) The following 10 lines stress the figures **1, 4, 5, 6,** and **7.** Test your mastery of these figures. Try for a **perfect** copy.

```
fr4f ju7j ft5f jy6j fr4f ju7j ft5f jy6j fr4f ju7j
for4 gnu7 bit5 dry6 nor6 flu7 hit5 try6 nor4 gnu7

nor 4 gnu 7 bit 5 sly 6 for 4 gnu 7 sit 5 fly 6
mar 4 flu 7 kit 5 dry 6 war 4 flu 7 hit 5 sly 6

11 men; 74 women; 14 boys; 47 girls; Total 146
47 men; 14 women; 74 boys; 11 girls; Total 146

5 and 7 and 4 and 6 and 1 and 41 and 65 and 175
7 and 5 and 6 and 4 and 7 and 14 and 56 and 715

4 and 7 and 5 and 6 and 1 and 14 and 56 and 517
1 and 6 and 4 and 7 and 5 and 41 and 65 and 175
```

LESSON 29

Aim: (*a*) To develop sustained typing skill by 5-Minute Timings.

(*b*) To learn to type **Business Letters—Indented Form.**

1. Machine Adjustments: See Lesson 2.

2. Warm-up: (5 Minutes) Copy the first two lines exactly as shown; then throw the carriage twice and type the sentence 10 times.

```
f@f j&j f£f j_j d/d k'k s"s l(l ;); ;%;
f@f j&j f£f j_j d/d k'k s"s l(l ;); ;%;

Our new Ajax Pencils are £6 a box less 5%.
```

3. Skill-Building Work: (20 Minutes)

(*a*) Preview Practice on Words and Phrases .... 3 minutes

(*b*) Two 1-Minute Timings and Word Practice .... 3 minutes

(*c*) Two 5-Minute Timings and Word Practice ....14 minutes

—

20 minutes

First: **Preview Practice.** Each word and phrase 3 times:

```
letter...inside...begins...second...centre...
margin...spaces...popular...closing...address...
business...indented...semi-block...paragraphs...
in the...of the...at the...and the
```

Second: **Machine Adjustments for Timed Typing.**

(*a*) Clear all tab stops.

(*b*) Set a Tab Stop 5 spaces from left margin.

(*c*) Set Line Space Gauge for **double** spacing.

Repeat sentence as many times as you can.

Third: **Two 1-Minute Timings.**

```
                    5
The most popular business letter forms are
      10                      15
indented, semi-block, and block.
```

Fourth: Two 5-Minute Timings.

5

    The most popular business letter forms are
      10
indented, semi-block, and block.
     15   20
    In the indented form, the second line of the
    25   30
inside address is indented five spaces; third line
    35   40
ten spaces. Paragraphs are indented five spaces.
     45   50
The closing is indented in steps of five spaces.
      55   60
This form is used for short and very short letters
      65
and typed in double spacing.
      70   75
    In the semi-block form, each line of the inside
      80   85
address begins at the margin. Paragraphs are indented
    90   95
five spaces. The closing is block.
            100   105
    In the block form, each line of the inside address
         110   115
and paragraphs begins at the left margin. The closing
      120   125
is block and begins at the centre of the paper.

4. New Work: (15 Minutes) Business Letter—Indented Form.

(*a*) Business letters are typed on printed letterheads usually 210 mm × 297 mm. To look attractive a letter should appear like a picture in a frame. You can turn out attractive letters by keeping these two points in mind:

1. Left and right margins should be almost equal. The right margin may be slightly less than the left.

2. Top and bottom margins should be almost equal. The bottom margin may be a little wider than the top.

(*b*) Business letters are of three lengths: short, average, long. Experience will teach you how to estimate the margins for attractive letter placement. Meanwhile, here is an easy placement guide to get you started:

Letters of About 100 Words

Pica Type 15-70-20-6
Elite Type 25-80-20-6

Remember these 3 placement points.

(1) The first two figures are the left and right margin stops— as usual.

(2) The figure 20 means that you type the date on line 20 from top edge of paper.

(3) The inside address is typed on line 6 from date.

Letters Over 100 Words

(1) Same margin stops.

(2) Same top margin.

(3) For every 25 words over 100, subtract 1 from 6—for spaces between date and inside address.

(*c*) Now, see the next page and study the model of a short Indented Form Business Letter. Learn the names of the parts of the letter and the spacing between the parts—both are indicated. Then insert an A4 sheet and copy the model—step by step.

Indented Form:

(*a*) Used for short and very short letters; typed in **double** spacing.

(*b*) Paragraphs are indented 5 spaces from left margin.

(*c*) Inside address and closing are indented in steps of 5 spaces.

(*d*) Placement Points: (15-70-20-6 (Pica); 25-80-20-6 (Elite). Copy the model letter following.

1st: Clear tab stop set for 5-Minute Timing.

2nd: Set new Tab Stops for inside address, paragraph beginnings, and the closing.

3rd: Set Line Space Gauge for **double** spacing.

Initials of dictator and typist	GH:HG 12th January, 19--.	Date line 10 double spaces from top. Backspace from right margin.

Inside address 3 double spaces from date.	Messrs. Harvey & Co.,
	    735 Hunter Avenue,
	        HULL
	            HU10 6EW.	

	Dear Sirs,	
Set Tab stop 5 spaces from left margin.	Under separate cover, we are mailing	One double space between lines and between paragraphs.
	to you one of our current catalogues.	
	When you are again in the market for	
	our products, we shall appreciate the	
	opportunity of submitting prices.	
Set Tab stop at centre.	Yours faithfully, MODERN HARDWARE COMPANY	Complimentary Close
	George Hayward Sales Manager	3 double spaces between firm name and name of dictator.

> **INDENTED FORM.** Used for short and very short letters.

5. Self-Testing Work: (30 Minutes) Here are three more very short letters. Type each one on a separate sheet, double-spaced, indented form—like the model on page 112.

```
        JHB:MS         5th February, 19--.

        Edgar Price, Esq.,
           350 Summer Street,
              LONDON SW1H OLF.

        Dear Sir,

             This is our third letter
        to you concerning your January
        account.

             We can hardly believe
        that you are trying to avoid
        payment.  Yet that is what we
        are forced to assume if you
        continue to neglect this
        matter.

                        Yours faithfully,
                        SMITH & WALTERS



                        John H. Banks
                        Credit Manager



        WW:JR          13th June, 19--.

        Albert Marshall, Esq.,
           720 High Street,
              PURLEY,
                 Surrey
                    CR2 4TJ.

        Dear Mr. Marshall,

             We expect to complete
        your order for writing paper
        by 15th June.
```

Your address has been
changed on our records to
agree with the one given in
your letter.

Yours sincerely,

William Winters
Sales Manager

HCB:SW   12th September, 19--.

Messrs. Martin & Dale,
     290 Arch Street,
        LONDON W1H 6AN.

Dear Sirs,

Thank you for your letter
of 9th September.

Our sales manager, Mr.
Wilson, will be glad to discuss the matter with your Mr.
Gordon at this office any day
next week between 2 p.m. and
4 p.m.

Yours faithfully,
BENTON & COMPANY

Harold C. Benton
Managing Director

6. Symbol Review: (5 Minutes) The following 12 lines stress @ £ __ &
to strengthen your control of these symbol keys. See how many **perfect** lines you can type.

f@f j&j f£f j_j f@f j&j f£f j_j f@f j&j f£f j_j f@f j&j
Lamps £4; Chairs £7; Tables £9; Desks £12;
Desks £9; Tables £8; Chairs £6; Lamps £10;

fr4f ju7j ft5f jy6j f4f j7j f5f j6j f@f j&j f£f j_j
50 @ £1 is £50.   25 @ £1 is £25.   20 @ £5 is £100
Dining-room; drawing-room; dining-room; drawing-room;

f@f j&j f£f j_j f@f j&j f£f j_j f@f j&j f£f j_j f@f j&j
We offer Zenith Television Sets @ £195.
We offer Bendix Television sets @ £190

f@f j&j f£f j_j f@f j&j f£f j_j f@f j&j f£f j_j f@f j_j
Philco & Company; Zenith & Company; Bendix & Company;
Zenith & Company; Bendix & Company; Philco & Company;

LESSON 30

Aim: (*a*) To develop sustained typing skill by 5-Minute Timings.

(*b*) To learn to type **Business Letters—Semi-block Form.**

1. Machine Adjustments: See Lesson 2.

2. Warm-up: (5 Minutes) Copy the first two lines exactly as shown; then throw the carriage twice and type the sentence 10 times.

```
frf juj ftf jyj fgf jhj ded kik sws lol aqa
fvf jmj fbf jnj dod k,k sxs l.l aza ;/; ;½;
We expect Vermont to yield large blocks of quartz.
```

3. Skill-Building Work: (20 Minutes)

(*a*) Preview Practice on Words and Phrases .... 3 minutes

(*b*) Two 1-Minute Timings and Word Practice .... 3 minutes

(*c*) Two 5-Minute Timings and Word Practice ....14 minutes

—

20 minutes

First: **Preview Practice.** Each word and phrase 3 times:

```
device...margin...simply...holding...machine...
already...extreme...desired...carriage...
tabulator...on the...to the...with the...
do not...you have
```

Second: **Machine Adjustments for Timed Typing.**

(*a*) Clear all tab stops.

(*b*) Set a Tab Stop 5 spaces from left margin.

(*c*) Set Line Space Gauge for **double** spacing.

Third: **Two 1-Minute Timings.**

```
               5                              10
    The tabulator key or bar is a labour-saving device.
              15                      20
By holding it down, you make the carriage jump to any
          24
point on the scale.
```

117

Fourth: **Two 5-Minute Timings.**

```
                      5                              10
     The tabulator key or bar is a labour-saving device.
                  15                      20
By holding it down, you make the carriage jump to any

point on the scale.
        25                      30
     First, of course, you have to clear the machine
        35                      40
of all tab stops that may already be set.  To do so,
    45                      50
move the left and right margin stops to the extreme
    55                      60
ends; then hold down the clear key and move the
        65                      70
carriage from side to side with the carriage release
    75
key.
                              80
     To set your own tab stops, move the carriage
        85                      90
to each desired point on the scale and press the set
    95
key.
```

4. New Work: (15 Minutes) Business Letter—Semi-block Form.

    (*a*) Inside address is blocked at the margin.

    (*b*) First line of each paragraph is indented 5 spaces.

    (*c*) Complimentary close, firm's name, dictator's name, are blocked.

Copy, step by step, the following model.

    1st: Clear tab stop set for 5-Minute Timing.

    2nd: Set one new Tab Stop 5 spaces from left margin; another at centre of paper for the closing—40 (Pica); 48 (Elite).

    3rd: Set Line Space Gauge for **single** spacing.

MG:RL   17th September, 19--.

Date on line 20 from top. Backspace from right margin.

Allen Clothing Company,
285 Webster Avenue,
LONDON W1R 5EE.

2 spaces between inside address and the salutation.

2 spaces between date and inside address.

Dear Sirs,

    Thank you for your cheque for £300, which has been credited to your account.

    It is not customary for us to grant extensions on accounts, as the terms indicated on the invoice are a definite part of our sales policy. We will make an exception in your case, however, because we believe that our delay in dispatching your order must have caused you some loss of sales.

2 spaces between paragraphs.

    We request that you co-operate with us by paying the balance of £215 by the first of next month. It would be wise for you to close this account to maintain your credit standing with the bank.

                    Very truly yours,
                    EXCLUSIVE CLOTHIERS, LTD.

                    Martin Goldsmith
                    Office Manager

SEMI-BLOCK FORM.   100 words. Placement Points: 15-70-20-6 (Pica)
                                                     25-80-20-6 (Elite)

5. Self-Testing Work: (30 Minutes) Type the following two letters in semi-block form (like the model on page 119). Arrange each on a separate sheet. Each letter contains about 100 words.

```
RC:HF                    4th October, 19--.

Messrs. Thomas Smith & Co.,
5 Wellington Road,
RICHMOND,
Surrey
TW9 1JA.

Dear Sir,

     We thank you for your inquiry
of 3rd October regarding discount
allowed on orders for our special
lines of furniture.

     On orders received from you
some years ago we allowed you a
special discount of five per cent.
We regret, however, that in
consequence of the present conditions
and the high cost of production, we
have been compelled to compile our
present catalogue on a strictly cash
basis.

     In these circumstances we are
sorry that we are unable to extend
to you the same concession as in the
past, but in order to meet you to some
extent we shall be pleased to allow
you a discount of five per cent on all
individual orders of £100 in value or
over.

                    Yours faithfully,
                    ACME FURNITURE COMPANY


                    Robert Carver
                    Manager
```

RC:HF   3rd November, 19--.

Messrs. Lawrence & Company,
431 Howard Street,
LONDON W1V 9RB.

Dear Sirs,

　　Thank you for your order of 29th October.
It seems to be the most substantial order you
have sent us since last October.

　　We appreciate this business very much and
hope that your sales will steadily increase
and thus give you a good start for the new year.
We assure you that we shall co-operate with you
by furnishing the finest workmanship and the
fastest service possible.

　　The chairs you refer to in your letter are
now being prepared for dispatch and they should
reach you by Tuesday, 6th November.

　　　　　　　　　　　　Very truly yours,
　　　　　　　　　　　　ACME FURNITURE COMPANY

　　　　　　　　　　　　Robert Carver
　　　　　　　　　　　　Manager

6. Symbol Review: (5 Minutes) The following 6 lines stress:
$/$ (slant); $\frac{1}{2}$ (one-half); - (hyphen).

d/d ;$\frac{1}{2}$; ;-; d/d ;$\frac{1}{2}$; ;-; d/d ;$\frac{1}{2}$; ;-; d/d ;$\frac{1}{2}$; ;-; d/d ;$\frac{1}{2}$; ;-;
The box measured 5$\frac{1}{2}$ x 4$\frac{1}{2}$ x 3$\frac{1}{2}$. Add $\frac{1}{2}$ and $\frac{1}{2}$; the sum is 1.

d/d ;$\frac{1}{2}$; ;-; d/d ;$\frac{1}{2}$; ;-; d/d ;$\frac{1}{2}$; ;-; d/d ;$\frac{1}{2}$; ;-; d/d ;$\frac{1}{2}$; ;-;
A figure 1$\frac{1}{2}$ by 1$\frac{1}{2}$ is a square. The table was 24$\frac{1}{2}$ by 10$\frac{1}{2}$.

d/d ;$\frac{1}{2}$; ;-; d/d ;$\frac{1}{2}$; ;-; d/d ;$\frac{1}{2}$; ;-; d/d ;$\frac{1}{2}$; ;-; d/d ;$\frac{1}{2}$; ;-;
His nephew had $\frac{1}{2}$ of his estate. Apples cost 3p each.

LESSON 31

Aim: (*a*) To develop sustained typing skill by 5-Minute Timings.

(*b*) To learn to type **Business Letters—Block Form.**

1. Machine Adjustments: See Lesson 2.

2. Warm-up: (5 Minutes) Copy the first two lines exactly as shown; then throw the carriage twice and type the sentence 10 times:

```
f4f j7j f5f j6j d3d k8k s2s 191 ;0; ;/; ;½; ;-;
f4f j7j f5f j6j d3d k8k s2s 191 ;0; ;/; ;½; ;-;
```

```
The sum of 10 and 29 and 38 and 47 and 56 and 7 is 187.
```

3. Skill-Building Work: (20 Minutes)

(*a*) Preview Practice on Words and Phrases .... 3 minutes

(*b*) Two 1-Minute Timings and Word Practice .... 3 minutes

(*c*) Two 5-Minute Timings and Word Practice ....14 minutes

—

20 minutes

First: **Preview Practice.** Each word and phrase 3 times:

```
typing...letter...writing...company...address...
printed...business...consists...outgoing...
wrinkled...therefore...letterhead...appearance...
attractive...responsible...correspondence...
in the...of the...and the...from the...that is
```

Second: **Machine Adjustments for Timed Typing.**

(*a*) Clear all tab stops.

(*b*) Set a Tab Stop 5 spaces from left margin.

(*c*) Set Line Space Gauge for **double** spacing.

Third: **Two 1-Minute Timings.**

```
                    5                          10
    In the business world, much of the typing consists
                  15                       20
of letter writing.  Outgoing business letters are typed
              25
on letterhead paper.
```

Fourth: **Two 5-Minute Timings.**

```
                        5                          10
    In the business world, much of the typing consists
                   15                    20
of letter writing.  Outgoing business letters are typed
                25                    30
on letterhead paper; that is, paper on which the company's
          35
name and address are printed.
               40                         45
    The letterhead paper used for business correspond-
          50                    55
ence is 210 mm wide and 297 mm long.  Plain paper
       60
is used for carbon copies.
          65                     70
    The typist is responsible for the appearance of
     75                    80
the letter.  The good typist, therefore, takes pains
     85                    90
to make every letter attractive.  The print should be
95                     100                     105
dark and even, and the type should be clean.  The paper
                110                    114
should be fresh - never soiled or wrinkled.
```

4. New Work: (15 Minutes) Business Letter—Block Form

    (*a*) Inside address is blocked at the margin.

    (*b*) Paragraphs are not indented.

    (*c*) Complimentary close, firm's name, dictator's name, are blocked.

Copy, step by step, the following model.

      1st: Clear the tab stop set for the 5-Minute Timing.

      2nd: Set a new Tab Stop at centre of paper: 40 (Pica); 48 (Elite).

      3rd: Set Line Space Gauge for **single** spacing.

LS:MB   18th February, 19--.

Inside   Messrs. James Thompson & Co.,
address   267 North Street,   4 spaces
6 spaces   LIVERPOOL,   between
from date.   Merseyside.   address and
                                                       salutation.

            Dear Sirs,

            Thank you for your letter of February
            15th, informing us that the consignment
            of boys' hats has not yet reached you.
            We regret this delay as much as you do.   2 spaces
                                                       between
            Our traffic manager has already   paragraphs.
            telephoned the railway authorities and
Body   has asked them to make immediate
of   enquiries. We understand they are doing
letter   this.

            If the hats do not reach you by February
            23rd, please let us know and we shall
            send you a duplicate consignment the same
            day.

                        Yours faithfully,
                        MARVIN HAT COMPANY

                                                       Last 4
                                                       lines at
                                                       centre.

                        Lawrence Smith
                        Manager

BLOCK FORM.   90 words. Placement Points: 15-70-20-6 (Pica)
                                            25-80-20-6 (Elite)
            Note the block inside address; block paragraph
            beginnings; block complimentary closing.

5. Self-Testing Work: (30 Minutes) See whether you can type following the letters. Arrange each on a separate sheet, in block form (like the model on page 124).

```
MB:HF                  23rd June, 19--.

Messrs. Robert Brown & Son,
179 Elm Street,
NOTTINGHAM.

Dear Sirs,

In response to your application,
we enclose a copy of our revised
price list.

From this you will see that
because of further saving in
manufacturing costs, made
possible by the introduction of
new machinery, we have been able
to announce a reduction in prices,
which will take effect on the
first of next month.

We believe that these reduced
prices will serve to encourage
the use of our products and we
look forward to the pleasure of
doing considerable business with
you during the forthcoming season.

                    Yours faithfully,
                    BROWN PAPER COMPANY



                    Martin Bradley
                    Manager


Enc.
```

Business Letter, Block Form - Alternative lay-out

RC:JH

2nd August, 19--.

James Barnett, Esq.,
385 Henry Street,
MOLD,
Flintshire CH2 4TJ.

Dear Sir,

Thank you very much for your
letter of the 27th expressing
your desire to open an account
with us. We are always glad
to welcome a new customer and
assure you of our desire to
serve you.

You are, of course, familiar
with forms such as the one
enclosed. All responsible
business firms use such forms
to secure information that may
facilitate the opening of an
account.

May we, therefore, trouble you
to complete this form and
return it to us in the enclosed
stamped envelope. We shall then
make the necessary inquiries to
hasten the opening of your account.

Yours faithfully,
JAMES ROBINSON & CO.

Raymond Cole
Manager

Enc.

6. Number Review: (5 Minutes) The following 10 lines stress the figures
2, 3, 8, 9, 0. See whether you can type a **perfect** copy.

de3d ki8k sw2s lo91 ;p0; de3d ki8k sw2s lo91 ;p0;
ire3 ski8 low2 two9 lip0 ire3 ski8 tow2 two9 lip0

3 and 8 and 2 and 9 and 0 and 9 and 8 and 3 and 2
8 and 3 and 2 and 0 and 9 and 3 and 9 and 8 and 2

29 and 38 and 90 and 83 and 92 and 20 and 80 and 30
20 and 83 and 93 and 82 and 29 and 38 and 92 and 80

Canal 2-9380; Castle 2-3928; Spring 3-2903; CA 5-2894
Axtel 8-0293; Spring 3-0329; Castle 9-3028; SP 8-0982

Rector 9-0932; Bryant 3-8032; Walker 8-3028; RE 2-0389
Oregon 3-0823; Oxford 2-2030; Lehigh 3-9089; OX 8-3290

LESSON 32

Aim: *(a)* To develop sustained typing skill by 5-Minute Timings.
     (b) To learn to type **2-Column Tabulations.**

1. Machine Adjustments: See Lesson 2.

2. Warm-up: (5 Minutes) Copy the first two lines exactly as shown;
then throw the carriage twice and type the sentence 10 times:

```
frf juj ded kik sws lol aqa ;p; fvf jmj fgf jhj fbf
dcd k,k sxs 1.1 aza fgf jhj fbf jnj fvf jmj dcd k,k

The quick, old judge admired the boy for his zeal.
```

3. Skill-Building Work: (20 Minutes)
    (a) Preview Practice on Words and Phrases .... 3 minutes
    (b) Two 1-Minute Timings and Word Practice .... 3 minutes
    (c) Two 5-Minute Timings and Word Practice ....14 minutes
                                                   20 minutes

First: **Preview Practice.** Each word and phrase 3 times:

```
typing...number...begins...column...between...
longest...material...vertical...subtract...fraction...
carriage...placement...remainder...backspace...
tabulation...understand...horizontal...in the...
of the...at that...on which...there is
```

Second: **Machine Adjustments for Timed Typing.**
    (a) Clear all tab stops.
    (b) Set a Tab Stop 5 spaces from left margin.
    (c) Set Line Space Gauge for **double** spacing.

Third: **Two 1-Minute Timings.**

Repeat sentence as many times as you can.

```
                 5
Tabulation means typing material in table form
   10              15         17
to make it easy to read and understand.
```

Fourth: Two 5-Minute Timings.

<pre>
                           5
     Tabulation means typing material in table form
      10   15
to make it easy to read and understand.
                    20   25
     For vertical placement, subtract the total number
                  30   35
of lines from 70 and divide the remainder by 2. The
               40   45
answer shows the line number on which the typing begins.
      50   55
If there is a fraction, ignore it.
                         60   65
     For horizontal placement, count the strokes in the
                    70   75
longest line in each column and add 6 spaces between
                  80   85
columns. The total shows the width of the tabulation.
                   90   95
     Centre the carriage; backspace half the width of
                    100   105
the tabulation; set your left margin at that point.
                   110   115
Tap out on the space bar the longest line in the first
             120   125
column plus 6 more between the first two columns and
             130   135
set a tab stop at that point. Do the same for all other
         140
columns.
</pre>

4. New Work: (15 Minutes) 2-Column Tabulation.

Tabulation means typing material in table form—to make it easy to read and understand. Let us work out, step by step, the following tabulation:

<pre>
                  SCHOOL SUBJECTS

          Algebra   Home Economics
          Arithmetic   Hygiene
          Biology   Italian
          Book-keeping   Latin
</pre>

Chemistry	Mechanical Drawing
Commercial Law	Music
English	Natural Science
French	Physics
Geometry	Spanish
German	Social Studies
Health Education	Trigonometry
Hebrew	Typewriting

First: **Machine Adjustments.**

    (*a*) Move margin stops to opposite ends.

    (*b*) Clear all tab stops.

    (*c*) Set Line Space Gauge for **single** spacing.

Second: Insert paper, top edge even with alignment scale.

Third: Determine **vertical placement**—for equal top and bottom margins:

    1. Count the typewritten lines. (13)

    2. Count the blank lines between the typewritten lines. (3)

    3. Add: 13 plus 3 is 16. The tabulation occupies 16 lines.

    4. Subtract 16 lines from 70—the total number of lines on an A4 sheet of typing paper. 16 from 70 is 54. The 54 remaining blank lines are divided in half—for equal top and bottom margins.

    5. Divide 54 by 2. Result: 27.

    6. Space 27 times from top edge of paper.

    7. Move the carriage to the centre of the paper—40 (Pica); 48 (Elite).

    8. Centre and type the heading—SCHOOL SUBJECTS. Then space down twice for the next step—horizontal placement.

Fourth: Determine **horizontal placement**—for equal left and right margins:

    1. For each column in the tabulation, draw a horizontal line:

    _____

    2. Write on the lines the number of letters and spaces in the longest line in each column:

          16   18

3. Between the lines, write the number of spaces to leave between the columns. Six spaces are equal to about a half-inch—an easy eye span in reading; so let us leave 6 spaces:

<u>   16   </u>   6   <u>   18   </u>

4. Add the figures in Step 3: 16 plus 6 plus 18 equals 40. The tabulation is 40 horizontal spaces.
5. Move carriage to centre of paper: 40 (Pica); 48 (Elite).
6. Backspace from the centre point one-half the total number of spaces—in this case, half of 40, 20; half of 48, 24. Set the left margin stop here.
7. Tap the space bar 16 times for the longest item in the first column plus 6 more for the spaces between the columns, a total of 22 spaces. Set your **tab stop** at this point for the second column.
8. Type the two columns across the paper, using the tabular bar or key to jump the carriage to the second column.

5. **Self-Testing Work:** (30 Minutes) See whether you can centre vertically and horizontally the following 3 tabulations. Arrange each on a separate sheet.

Problem 1. (Centre on an A4 sheet of paper)

PRINCIPAL ENGLISH CITIES

London	Sheffield
Birmingham	Manchester
Nottingham	Norwich
Leeds	Bradford
Newcastle-upon-Tyne	Bristol
Darlington	Dover
Liverpool	Coventry
Bolton	Peterborough
Southampton	Plymouth
Portsmouth	Leicester
Crewe	Derby

Problem 2. (Centre on a half sheet of paper)
> NOTE: A half sheet of A4 typing paper accommodates 35 lines from top to bottom.

TEN ENGLISH COUNTIES

Essex	Cornwall
Hertfordshire	Derbyshire
Sussex	Yorkshire
Suffolk	Lancashire
Devon	Rutland

Problem 3. (Centre on a half sheet of paper)

PRINCIPAL RIVERS

Nile	Mackenzie
Amazon	Mekong
Mississippi-Missouri	Amur
Yangtze	Hwang Ho
Lena	Niger
Congo	Yenisey

6. Symbol Review: (5 Minutes) The following 9 lines stress:
" (Quotation Marks); / (Slant); ' (Apostrophe).
Aim for a **perfect** copy.

If keys lock, press margin release.

```
f@f j&j j_j d/d k'k s"s d/d s"s d/d k'k s"s d/d k'k
d/d k'k s"s d/d k'k s"s d/d k'k d/d s"s k'k d/d s"s

Boys' shoes; men's shirts; girls' dresses; ladies' hose
Men's boots; boys' slacks; girls' jackets; ladies' hose

f@f j&j j_j d/d k'k s"s d/d s"s d/d k'k s"s d/d k'k
d/d k'k s"s d/d k'k s"s d/d k'k d/d s"s k'k d/d s"s

d/d s"s k'k d/d s"s k'k d/d s"s k'k d/d s"s k'k d/d
Ben's car, a "Ford", is in front of Joe's house.
Jim's car, a "Vauxhall", is in front of Ken's house.
```

LESSON 33

Aim: (*a*) To develop sustained typing skill by 5-Minute Timings.

(*b*) To learn **3-Column Tabulation.**

1. Machine Adjustments: See Lesson 2.

2. Warm-up: (5 Minutes) Copy the first two lines exactly as shown; then throw the carriage twice and type the sentence 10 times.

```
frf juj ded kik sws lol aqa ;p; fvf jmj fbf jnj frf
dcd k,k sxs l.l aza ;%; ;½; ;-; ;½; ;-; frf juj ded
```

The puzzled judge was vexed at the quarrelsome witness.

3. Skill-Building Work: (20 Minutes)

(*a*) Preview Practice on Words and Phrases .... 3 minutes

(*b*) Two 1-Minute Timings and Word Practice .... 3 minutes

(*c*) Two 5-Minute Timings and Word Practice ....14 minutes

————

20 minutes

First: **Preview Practice.** Each word and phrase 3 times:

```
success...quality...holding...letting...ability...
shifted...between...failures...ordinary...dislodge...
pluggers...stickers...knuckling...you can...to that...
on the...you will...and the
```

Second: **Machine Adjustments for Timed Typing.**

(*a*) Clear all tab stops.

(*b*) Set a Tab Stop 5 spaces from left margin.

(*c*) Set Line Space Gauge for **double** spacing.

Third: **Two 1-Minute Timings.**

```
                        5
    You can make your life a success if you take hold
10                      15                           20
and never let go.  Most men and women owe their success
                      25      27
to that quality of holding on.
```

133

Fourth: Two 5-Minute Timings.

                          5
       You can make your life a success if you take hold
10   15   20
and never let go. Most men and women owe their success
                   25   30
to that quality of holding on; while most, if not all,
                   35
failures result from letting go.
                   40   45
       Success comes from knuckling down to hard work
              50   55
and being on the job every day. The best jobs are
              60   65
held by ordinary people - who won't let go.
                   70   75
       You will find failures in the ranks of men and
                        80   85
women of more than ordinary ability. They shifted
                        90   95
jobs so often that they could not get a hold on any job.
                   100   105
By the time they were ready to settle down, they found
              110   115   117
they could not dislodge the pluggers and the stickers.

4. New Work: (15 Minutes) 3-Column Tabulation.

Planning and typing a 3-column tabulation is almost the same as planning and typing a 2-column tabulation. The only difference is that you set two tab stops (one for the second column, one for the third column). As before, leave 6 blank spaces between columns. Let us work out, step by step, the following tabulation:

NEW YORK'S TALLEST BUILDINGS

Empire State	Metropolitan Life	Singer
Chrysler	Chanin	U.S. Court House
60 Wall Tower	Lincoln	Municipal
Chase Manhattan Bank	Irving Trust	Continental Bank
R.C.A.	General Electric	Sherry-Netherland
Woolworth	Waldorf-Astoria	Socony-Mobil
City Bank	10 East 40th Street	New York Central
500 Fifth Avenue	New York Life	Transportation

First: **Machine Adjustments.**

    (*a*) Move margin stops to opposite ends.

    (*b*) Clear all tab stops.

    (*c*) Set Line Space Gauge for single spacing.

Second: Insert paper, top edge even with alignment scale.

Third: Determine **vertical placement**—for equal top and bottom margins. Follow these steps:

1. Count the typewritten lines. (9)
2. Count the blank lines between the typewritten lines. (3)
3. Add: 9 plus 3 is 12. The tabulation occupies 12 lines.
4. Subtract 12 lines from 60—the total number of lines on a quarto sheet of typing paper. 12 from 60 is 48. The 48 remaining blank lines are divided in half—for equal top and bottom margins.
5. Divide 48 by 2. Result: 24.
6. Space 24 times from top edge of paper.
7. Move the carriage to the centre of the paper—40 (Pica); 48 (Elite).
8. Centre and type the heading—NEW YORK'S TALLEST BUILD-INGS. Then space down twice for the next step—horizontal placement.

Fourth: Determine **horizontal placement** for equal left and right margins. Follow these steps:

1. For each column in the tabulation, draw a horizontal line:

———————————   ———————————   ———————————

2. Write on the lines the number of letters and spaces in the longest item in each column:

  20   19   17
———————————   ———————————   ———————————

3. Between the lines, write the number of spaces to leave between the columns. As before, leave 6 spaces:

  20   6   19   6   17
———————————   ———————————   ———————————

4. Add the figures in step 3:

    20 + 6 + 19 + 6 + 17 = 68

The tabulation is 68 horizontal spaces.

5. Move the carriage to the centre of the paper: 40 (Pica); 48 (Elite).
6. Backspace from the centre point one-half the total number of spaces—in this case, half of 68, 34; and set the left margin stop here.
7. Tap the space bar 20 times—for the longest item in the first column plus 6 more for the spaces between the first and second columns, a total of 26 spaces. Set a **tab stop** at this point for the second column.
8. Tap the space bar 19 times—for the longest item in the second column plus 6 more for the spaces between the second and third columns, a total of 25 spaces. Set a **tab stop** at this point for the third column.
9. Type the three columns across the paper, using the tabular bar or key to jump the carriage from column to column as each line is typed.

5. **Self-Testing Work:** (30 Minutes) See how well you can centre the following 3 tabulations. Arrange each on a separate sheet.

Problem 1. (Centre on a quarto sheet of paper)

WORLD'S LARGEST COUNTRIES

Russia	Argentina	Iran
Canada	Sudan	Mongolia
China	Fr. Equatorial Africa	Saudi Arabia
Brazil	Belgian Congo	Indonesia
United States	Algeria	Alaska
Australia	Greenland	Peru
Fr. West Africa	Mexico	Angola
India	Libya	Union of S. Africa

Problem 2. (Centre on a half sheet of paper)

REMINDER: A half sheet of quarto typing paper accommodates 30 lines from top to bottom.

EXPRESSIONS WRITTEN AS ONE WORD

today	without	classroom
tonight	inasmuch	beforehand
tomorrow	somewhat	standpoint
together	within	likewise
herein	everybody	roadway
hardware	meanwhile	postmaster
tryout	something	herewith

Problem 3. (Centre on a half sheet of paper)

WORDS FREQUENTLY MISSPELT

absence	chargeable	maintenance
absolutely	convenient	noticeable
accessible	correspondent	occurred
accidentally	counterfeit	pageant
accrued	customary	pamphlet
acquaintance	dependent	procedure
allotted	discipline	questionnaire
apparently	distinguished	recommend
assistance	eligible	religious
associate	embarrass	restaurant

6. Symbol Review: (5 Minutes) The following 12 lines stress:
( ) (Parentheses); ? (Question Mark); : (Colon).
Copy them exactly as shown.

```
1(1 ;); ;?; ;:; 1(1 ;); ;?; ;:; 1(1 ;); ;?; ;:;
The lease read:  Rental to be Forty Pounds (£40).
The lease read:  Rental to be Sixty Pounds (£60).

How much?  How soon?  How many?  How good?  How often?
Where is Maxim?  Do you think he is in the auditorium?
Where is Frank?  Do you think he is in the laboratory?

1(1 ;); ;?; ;:; 1(1 ;); ;?; ;:; 1(1 ;); ;?; ;:;
Dr. Zinman will be in his office today at 10.15 a.m.
Dr. Saxton will be in his office today at 12.30 p.m.

The price of "America" (1953 edition) now is £2.
The price of "Victory" (1948 edition) now is £2·50.
The price of "Germany" (1952 edition) now is £3.
```

LESSON 34

Aim: (*a*) To develop sustained typing skill by 5-Minute Timings.

(*b*) To learn **3-Column Tabulations** with **Column Headings**.

1. Machine Adjustments: See Lesson 2.

2. Warm-up: (5 Minutes) Copy the first two lines exactly as shown; then throw the carriage twice and type the sentence 10 times:

```
frf juj ftf jyj fgf jhj fbf jnj fvf jmj ded kik
aqa ;p; dod k,k sxs l.l aqa aqa ;p; aza sxs l.l
```

```
Six or seven flashing new jet planes quickly zoomed by.
```

3. Skill-Building Work: (20 Minutes)

(*a*) Preview Practice on Words and Phrases .... 3 minutes

(*b*) Two 1-Minute Timings and Word Practice .... 3 minutes

(*c*) Two 5-Minute Timings and Word Practice ....14 minutes

                                                     ——

                                                20 minutes

First: **Preview Practice.** Each word and phrase 3 times:

```
worked...quit...trying...better...amount...future...
always...change...decided...another...building...
finished...realized...interested...accomplished...
at the...he had...to do....did not...it is
```

Second: **Machine Adjustments for Timed Typing.**

(*a*) Clear all tab stops.

(*b*) Set a Tab Stop 5 spaces from left margin.

(*c*) Set Line Space Gauge for **double** spacing.

Third: **Two 1-Minute Timings.**

```
                       5
    When Henry Ford was making his first car in a
     10                        15
small brick building at the rear of his home, he
     20              23
worked day and night.
```

Fourth: **Two 5-Minute Timings.**

5
When Henry Ford was making his first car in a
10   15

small brick building at the rear of his home, he

     20   25

worked day and night. He was very much interested

    30   35

in what he was trying to create. When he had finished

  40   45

it, his interest waned. He felt he had accomplished

50   55

what he had set out to do.

60
But he began to think. He realized that if he
65   70

quit now, and did not try to build a better car than

 75   80   85

his first one, his life would not amount to much. So

      90   95

he decided to start right away to make a better car.

     100   105

He saw a future for his car, and so he went to work

    110   115

again with all his might, and made a car better than

his first.

120   125
It is always too soon to quit. Change your plans,
130   135   138

if you must, make another start, but never quit.

4. New Work: (15 Minutes) 3-Column Tabulation with Column Headings. Planning and typing a 3-column tabulation with column headings is almost the same as planning and typing a 3-column tabulation without column headings. The only difference is that you centre the column headings over the columns. Let us work out, step by step, the following tabulation:

FAMOUS WORLD EXHIBITIONS

Exhibition	Year	Place
The Great Exhibition	1851	London
Louisiana Purchase	1904	St. Louis

```
Panama-Pacific              1915    San Francisco
Century of Progress         1933    Chicago

New York World's Fair       1939    New York
Festival of Britain         1951    London
```

First: **Machine Adjustments.**
    (*a*) Move margin stops to opposite ends.
    (*b*) Clear all tab stops.
    (*c*) Set Line Space Gauge for single spacing.

Second: Insert paper, top edge even with alignment scale.

Third: Determine **vertical placement**—for equal top and bottom margins. Follow these steps:

1. Count the typewritten lines. (8)
2. Count the blank lines between the typewritten lines. (4)
3. Add: 8 plus 4 is 12. The tabulation occupies 12 lines.
4. Subtract 12 lines from 70—the total number of lines on an A4 sheet of typing paper. 12 from 70 is 58. The 58 remaining blank lines are divided in half—for equal top and bottom margins.
5. Divide 58 by 2. Result: 29.
6. Space 29 times from top edge of paper.
7. Move the carriage to the centre of the paper: 40 (Pica); 48 (Elite).
8. Centre and type the main heading—FAMOUS WORLD EXHIBITIONS.
    Then space down 4 times for the next step—horizontal placement.
    NOTE: You will centre the column headings after you have typed the body of the tabulation.

Fourth: Determine **horizontal placement**—for equal left and right margins.

    1. For each column in the tabulation, draw a horizontal line.

_____   _____   _____

2. Write on the lines the number of letters and spaces in the longest item in each column:

21	4	13

3. Between the lines, write the number of spaces to leave between the columns. As before, leave 6 spaces:

21	6	4	6	13

4. Add the figures in Step 3.

$$21 + 6 + 4 + 6 + 13 = 50$$

5. Move the carriage to the centre of the paper—40 (Pica); 48 (Elite).

6. Backspace from the centre point one-half the total number of spaces—in this case, half of 50, 25; and set the left margin stop here.

7. Tap the space bar 21 times—for the longest item in the first column plus 6 more for the spaces between the first and second columns—a total of 27 spaces. Set a **tab stop** at this point for the second column.

8. Tap the space bar 4 times—for the longest item in the second column plus 6 more for the spaces between the second and third columns—a total of 10 spaces. Set your **tab stop** at this point for the third column.

9. Now type the 3 columns across the paper—using the tabulator bar or key—to jump the carriage from column to column as each line is typed.

10. Centre the column headings—as follows:
    (*a*) Roll the paper back to the main heading.
    (*b*) Space down twice from the main heading—for the column headings.
    (*c*) Move the carriage to the centre of the first column. Backspace **once** for every two letters in *Exhibition*. Then type the word and underscore it.

The centre of a column is half the number of spaces in the longest item.

    (*d*) Jump the carriage to the first **tab stop.** Type the word *Year* and underscore it.

    (*e*) Move the carriage to the centre of the third column. Backspace **once** for every two letters in *Place*. Then type the word and underscore it.

5. Self-Testing Work: (30 Minutes) Here are two more 3-column tabulations with column headings. Arrange each on an A4 sheet of paper.

Problem 1.

MONTHLY GENERAL RAINFALL

Month	Percentage of Averages England and Wales	Scotland
January	71	49
February	49	54
March	13	24
April	57	76
May	103	107
June	78	124
July	78	108
August	79	139
September	37	73
October	120	144
November	232	130
December	190	168

Problem 2.

FIRE LOSSES IN MARCH

Risk	Locality	Estimated Loss
Golf Club	Swindon	£3,000
Timber Yard	Torquay	£10,000
Theatre	Rochester	£5,000
Chemical Works	Birmingham	£12,000

Cloth Warehouse	Leeds	£5,000
Grocer	Stratford	£3,000
Private House	London	£1,500
Farm	Dorset	£4,500
Piano Factory	East Ham	£6,500
Warehouse	Bethnal Green	£10,350
Sawmill	Broxbourne	£5,300

6. Symbol Review: (5 Minutes) The following 12 lines stress:
@ (At); $\frac{1}{4}$ (One-quarter); % (Per cent).
Copy them exactly as shown:

```
;@; ;¼; ;%; ;@; ;¼; ;%; ;@; ;¼; ;%; ;@; ;¼; ;%;
The invoice read:  75 pairs @ 5% discount.
The invoice read:  80 pairs @ 3% discount.

;@; ;¼; ;%; ;@; ;¼; ;%; ;@; ;¼; ;%; ;@; ;¼; ;%;
The bank increased the interest rate from 2¼% to 3¼%.
The bank increased the interest rate from 3¼% to 4¼%.

;@; ;¼; ;%; ;@; ;¼; ;%; ;@; ;¼; ;%; ;@; ;¼; ;%;
The symbols @ and % are often used in statements.
The symbols @ and % are often used in statements.

;@; ;¼; ;%; ;@; ;¼; ;%; ;@; ;¼; ;%; ;@; ;¼; ;%;
The asterisk is frequently used for footnotes.
The asterisk is frequently used for footnotes.
```

SUPPLEMENTS

SUPPLEMENTS

1.

COMMON ERRORS AND HOW TO OVERCOME THEM

Here are some of the errors you may make until your typing skill is fully developed. You can easily avoid these errors by studying the cause and improving the technique suggested for remedying them:

TYPE OF ERROR	PROBABLE CAUSE	SUGGESTED REMEDY
1. Omission of space.	Typing too fast.	Slow down a bit. Type with better control of your fingers.
2. Too many spaces.	Pushing the space bar.	Strike the space bar sharply, as though it were red hot.
3. Shadowed letters.	Pushing the keys.	Strike each key with the fingertip sharply. Release instantly.
4. Omitted letters.	Typing too fast.	Slow down a bit. Type with better control of your fingers. Spell the words as you type.
5. Raised capital letters.	Releasing the shift key too soon.	Hold the shift key until you have struck the letter key.
6. Omitted or inserted words.	Losing your place in the copy.	Keep your eyes on the copy, even when throwing the carriage for a new line.
7. Uneven left margin.	Throwing the carriage too slowly or too sharply.	Practise throwing the carriage with the same force after each line.

2.

PUNCTUATION SPACING

RULE	*Example*

1. Space Once—

(a) After a comma.	We need eggs, butter, and milk.
(b) After a semicolon.	Taste it; you may like it.
(c) After the full stop in an abbreviation.	Mr. and Mrs. Weston have arrived.
(d) Between a whole number and a 'made' fraction.	The road is 5 1/2 kilometres long. (BUT: The road is $5\frac{1}{2}$ kilometres long.)
(e) Before and after the ampersand.	Mary is a cashier at the May & Co. store.
(f) Before and after a dash.	Every champion was once a beginner - with ambition.

2. Space Twice—

(a) After the full stop at the end of a sentence.	John Jenkins was born in Shepperton. When he was five he lived in Leeds.
(b) After a colon.	The teacher said: "Strike the keys with the fingertips."
(c) After the exclamation mark.	What! Haven't you finished it yet?

3. Do Not Space—

(a) Between parentheses and the words they enclose.	Mr. Van Dusen (book-keeper) opened the safe.
(b) Between quotation marks and the words they enclose.	Franklin D. Roosevelt said: "The one thing we have to fear is fear itself."
(c) Before or after the hyphen in compound words.	His brother-in-law is in the Navy.

(*d*) Before or after a decimal point.	The bonds yield 3.5% interest.
(*e*) Before or after a comma in numerals.	The sun is 1,305,000 times as large as the earth.
(*f*) Before or after the apostrophe.	Joe's car is in the garage.
(*g*) Before the % symbol.	Savings Banks pay 3½% interest.
(*h*) Before or after the full stop in time of day.	Our train leaves at 1.30 p.m.

3.

RULES FOR DIVIDING WORDS AT THE END OF A LINE

1. Divide a word only between syllables.
   EXAMPLES: con-tain, pro-gramme, trans-act.
2. Divide a word between consonants.
   EXAMPLES: let-ter, rub-ber, begin-ning.
   But: If a word is derived from a word ending in a double conso-
   nant, divide after the second consonant:
   EXAMPLES: tall-est, add-ing.
3. Divide a word after the prefix.
   EXAMPLES: be-tween, sub-mit, dis-appoint.
4. Divide a word before the suffix.
   EXAMPLES: lov-ing, judg-ment.
5. Divide a hyphenated word only on the hyphen.
   EXAMPLES: self-confidence, attorney-general.
   NOTE: All words beginning with *self* are hyphenated,
   except **selfish.**
6. Do not divide a word of one syllable.
   EXAMPLES: please, height, through.
7. Do not carry over ed, er, ly. Finish the word.
   EXAMPLES: tested, rather, lovely.
8. Do not divide proper names.
   EXAMPLES: George, Friday, Perth.

9. Do not separate the title from the name.
   EXAMPLES: Mr. Hudson, Dr. Miller.
10. Do not divide figures, contractions, or abbreviations.
    EXAMPLES: £2,500,000; C. O. D.; wasn't; 7.30 p.m.
11. Do not divide four letter words.
    EXAMPLES: only, rely, upon.
12. Do not divide the last word on a page.
13. Do not divide the last word in a paragraph.
    NOTE: When in doubt, find out. **Consult the Dictionary.**

4.

FACILITY SENTENCE PRACTICE

Repeated practice of the following sentences will boost your typing speed. Type each sentence 10 times.

Margin Stops: For **Pica** Type .... 15 and 70.
                For **Elite** Type .... 25 and 80.

	5-Stroke Words
1. Mix work with pluck - for luck.	6
2. Every champion was once a beginner.	7
3. The empty can makes the most noise.	7
4. Try to be thorough in everything you do.	8
5. Money is most useful when it circulates.	8
6. An expert is one who excels in his work.	8
7. If you look for trouble, you will find fault.	9
8. A good way to win an argument is to avoid it.	9
9. To win friends, show yourself to be friendly.	9
10. Be a live wire; then no one will step on you.	9
11. The dumb person is one who is always talking.	9

12. You must pay the price to excel in your work. 9

13. Talk may be cheap but not over the telephone. 9

14. To make good, you must have the will to make good. 10

15. A grudge is too heavy a load for any man to carry. 10

16. The world pays very well to those who really know. 10

17. Never try to get even; better strive to get ahead. 10

18. Help your fellow workers if you want to be helped. 10

19. You cannot see the future, but it is always before you. 11

20. Your mind is like a parachute; it works only when open. 11

1   2   3   4   5   6   7   8   9   10   11

5.

ALPHABETIC SENTENCE PRACTICE

Alphabetic sentences are very useful for review and for obtaining a thorough command of the keyboard. Each of the following sentences contains every letter of the alphabet. Repeated thoughtful typing of these sentences will help you master the keyboard and make you a skilful typist.

DIRECTIONS

1. Machine Adjustments.

(*a*) Clear all tab stops.

(*b*) Set Margin Stops: For **Pica** Type .... at 15 and 70.

                        For **Elite** Type .... at 25 and 80.

(*c*) Set a Tab Stop 5 spaces from your left margin.

(*d*) Set Line Space Gauge for **single** spacing.

2. Practice Procedure.

(*a*) Type the first sentence 5 times.

(*b*) Check your work. Make a list of the words in which you find errors.

(*c*) Practise each word until you can type it smoothly and accurately.

(*d*) Type the sentence again 5 times. Aim for greater accuracy.

NOTE: (*a*) Try two sentences each day.
   (*b*) When you have tried them all, repeat this procedure.

                    5
1.   Joseph Boxer packed my sledge with seventy two
         10
quails.

                    5
2.   Peter Fahb quickly mixed two jugs of liquid
     10   11
veneer.

                    5
3.   The job requires extra pluck and zeal from every
     10   13
young wage earner.

                    5
4.   The jovial chemist quickly analysed the mixture
       10   14
of green and brown powder.

                    5
5.   The queer, lazy witness from Kansas vexed the
         10   14
capable, patient old judge.

                    5   10
6.   John Wilborg, trapeze artist, executed his famous
                    15
jumping act very quickly.

                    5
7.   Joe Quick, brainy government expert, was amazed
       10   15   18
to find numerous errors in the tax report.

                    5
8.   You can make good on your job and even excel in
       10   15   19
your work if you perform every task with quiet zeal.

                    5
9.   Our laboratory has just developed an amazing new
       10   15   20
wax that quickly restores the original finish on all
              22
furniture.

<pre>
                            5
10.   John Quinn improved his typewriting skill by
           10   15
     seizing every opportunity to practise effective speed-
        20   23
     building exercises.
</pre>

6.

ACCURACY AND SPEED PRACTICE

Accuracy and speed will come to you with thoughtful repetition practice. Devote a definite amount of time for practice each day. To reach your highest speed and accuracy, constantly keep in mind the following points:

1. Strike each key only with the finger that controls it. Strike the keys squarely in the centre, quickly and sharply.
2. Keep your fingers curved like claws—close to the home keys.
3. Move your fingers only. Keep arms and elbows close to your sides.
4. Type by touch only. Keep your eyes on the copy—even when throwing the carriage for a new line.
5. Type the common words as a unit, not letter by letter. For example, when typing the word **the**, don't spell it to yourself (**t-h-e**). Think of it and type it as a unit (**the**). Form this habit, and you will soon be a faster and more accurate typist.

7.

HOW TO USE THE 5-MINUTE TIMED TESTS
(Pages 151, 152, 153)

1. Use them for practise and for timing. Aim for **speed** and **accuracy**.
2. Set Margin Stops at 15 and 70 (Pica); 25 and 80 (Elite).
   Set a Tab Stop 5 spaces from your left margin.
   Set Line Space Gauge for **double** spacing.
3. Type each paragraph in a selected test twice; then time yourself for 5 minutes on the entire copy. When you have tried every test, start over again from the beginning.
4. Check your work. List the words in which you find errors. Practise each word until you can type it smoothly and accurately.

5. If you have difficulty with certain letters, practise the appropriate Corrective Drill in Supplement 8.

REMINDER: (1) Take two 5-Minute tests on the same copy.

(2) Determine your typing speed in correct words per minute on each test.

(3) Enter the better of the two scores in your Personal Progress Record which you started in Lesson 15.

MEANING OF CREDIT

```
                              5
        Credit is the power of obtaining something today
 10                          15                        20
in return for future payment.  When you buy supplies
                             25
at a store to be paid for on the first of the
      30                          35
following month, credit is used.
                             40                          45
        Credit is confidence that the borrower will repay.
                             50                    55
This confidence rests upon the character of the borrower
                   60                   65
and his ability and willingness to pay at a definite

time.
                   70                        75
        About 10 per cent of business is carried on by
                   80                        85
cash; about 90 per cent is carried on by credit through
             90
the use of credit instruments.
         95                          100
        Cheques, notes, bonds, are a few examples of credit
 105                         110                        115
instruments.  They serve as substitutes for money and
                        120                       125
do away with the need for a vast amount of actual money
                   130                   134
which would be required without their use.
```

Repeat if you finish before end of 5 minutes.

TODID IS HERE

5
Today is here. Do not waste time; the time you
10   15   20
wasted yesterday is lost forever. Do not worry about
        25
what may happen. Do the things you should do.
    30   35
Today is here. Do not look back at the past.
    40   45
Look forward. Do not imagine what you would do if
     50   55
things were different. You can make good with the
      60
assets you have.

         65   70
Today is here. Be kind to people; avoid hurting
         75   80
them. Look for good qualities, not faults. People,
       85
not things, are most important.
       90   95
Today is here. Study to improve yourself, for
        100   105
you should be prepared. It is the surest way to
succeed.
      110   115
Today is here. Make the most of it. Do not
      120   125
wait for tomorrow. Tomorrow never comes.

Repeat if you finish before end of 5 minutes.

LETTER WRITING

5
Every business letter you receive gives you an
10   15
impression of two people - the person who signed it

20   25
and the person who typed it. This applies to the
30
letters you type.
          35   40
     You may not be responsible for the way the
               45   50
letter is composed - the way in which the dictator
               55   60
has expressed his thoughts; but you are responsible
               65
for its typewritten appearance.
               70   75
     Make your letters look attractive. You can do
               80   85
so by accurate typing, artistic placement, correct
               90   95
grammar, spelling, and punctuation. If something in
               100   105
the letter does not seem to make sense, ask the dic-
               110
tator about it.
                         115
     Every office requires its letters to be typed
     120   125
according to certain standard letter forms. The
     130   135
three most popular forms are known as indented, semi-
     140   145
block and block. Models of these forms are in this
150
book.

Repeat if you finish before end of 5 minutes.

8.

CORRECTIVE DRILLS

a
drill   aboard absent absorb accept actual action advice

b
drill   bought belong behave before beauty battle basket

c
drill   carpet charge common copies coming church change

d
drill   design detail devote direct depend depart dances

e
drill   effort employ enjoys entire escape effect either

f
drill   future friend Friday forget follow finish filled

g
drill   ground glance giving garage garter gather gently

h
drill   handle happen height honest houses hungry hotels

i
drill   import indeed impose inborn income Indian indent

j
drill   jacket jungle juggle jumble joined jovial judges

k
drill   kettle kidnap kindly knight knives knotty knaves

l
drill   larger lately lawful lavish ledger letter liable

m
drill   member mental method middle mighty mailed manner

n
drill   notice ninety number nerves native narrow neatly

o
drill   object oblige offers orange origin outlet overdo

p
drill   pencil parcel parade parent papers pamper patent

q
drill   quaint Quaker quarts quench quotes quoted quotas

r
drill   reduce razors reader reason record region remote

```
s
drill     search second scheme sample salute silver saucer

t
drill     tender theory tavern temper thread thrift throng

u
drill     umpire uncles unique unlike untold unpack unload

v
drill     vanity valise vacant valley vanish virtue visits

w
drill     weight waited warmed wasted weapon weaver wheels

x
drill     excuse excite excess except exceed exhale exists

y
drill     yachts yellow yields yearly yonder yelled yawned

z
drill     zenith zipper zigzag zephyr zebras zealot zoning
```

9.

ERASING

Erasing wastes time. You can type 20 words in the time required to make one neat erasure, and many more if carbon copies are involved. So strive for accuracy. However, even the expert typist occasionally makes an error; so you should know how to make erasures neatly.

To Make a Neat Erasure:

1. Be sure your hands and eraser are clean. Clean the eraser by rubbing it briskly on white paper, or on fine-grained sandpaper.
2. Move the carriage to the left or right to prevent erasure grit from falling into the machine.
3. Roll the paper up until the error to be erased is on top of the roller. Hold the paper firmly by pressing it against the roller with your fingertips.
4. Erase the error with a light, short, circular motion, blowing lightly to keep the grit out of the machine.

5. Return the paper to the typing position and strike the correct letter lightly; then backspace and strike it again until the letter is as dark as the other letters on the sheet.

NOTE: 1. Use a typewriter eraser on the original copy; a soft pencil eraser on carbon copies.
2. Protect carbon copies from smudging by placing a small piece of paper under each carbon paper.
3. Erase on the top copy first; then remove one piece of protective paper at a time and erase the carbon copies.

10.
SPECIAL SYMBOLS

SYMBOL	HOW MADE	EXAMPLE
Dash —	Strike the hyphen. Space once before and after the dash.	Every champion was once a beginner - with ambition.
Exclamation Mark !	1. Strike the apostrophe. 2. Backspace. 3. Strike the full stop lightly.	Fight for your rights!
Multiplication Sign ×	Strike the small ×. Space once before and after the ×. In measurements, the × means BY.	5 x 10 a 9 x 15 rug.
Minus Sign —	Strike the hyphen. Space once before and after the minus sign.	12 - 5
Division Sign ÷	1. Strike the hyphen. 2. Backspace. 3. Strike the colon. Space once before and after the division sign.	20 ÷ 5

SYMBOL	HOW MADE	EXAMPLE
Plus Sign +	1. Strike the hyphen, then backspace. 2. Depress the shift lock, then strike the apostrophe. 3. Backspace, turn the roller up slightly, then strike the apostrophe again. (*Some typewriters have* + *signs, but many do not.*) Space once before and after the plus sign.	6 + 8
Equals Sign =	1. Strike the hyphen. 2. Backspace. 3. Turn the roller up slightly and strike the hyphen again. Space once before and after the equals sign.	5 x 10 = 50
Fractions not on the keyboard	Use the slant. Space once before and after the fraction.	5 1/3 7/8 of a kilo- metre
Ditto Mark "	Use quotation mark.	March 15 " 20
Caret √	1. Underscore preceding letter. 2. Strike slant in space between words.	him I saw/there
Degree Sign °	Turn the roller down slightly and strike the small o.	85°

Exponents (Raised numbers)	Turn the roller down slightly and strike the desired number.	x^2
Chemical Symbols (Lowered numbers)	Turn the roller up slightly and strike the desired number.	H_2O

11.
ADDRESSING ENVELOPES

1. Use double spacing for a three line address and single line spacing for an address of four lines or more.
2. Address may be typed in either block or indented form.
3. Type annotations such as 'Attention', 'Personal', on the left top corner of the envelope.

12.
MODES OF ADDRESS

When writing to someone who is entitled to various combinations of letters after his name, it is important to get these letters in the correct sequence. A person must be addressed by some form of title, e.g. Sir, Captain, Mr. (or Esq.)

They should appear in this order:

1. Title
2. Orders and decorations
3. University degrees
4. Distinctions, etc.

Mnemonic: Conferred by Crown, University, any other.
Note: V.C. (Victoria Cross)—most distinguished of all decorations and precedes everything.
Example: Sir John Smith, V.C., K.C.B., D.S.O., M.A., M.P.
Titles

Miss	(complete word)—no stop
Mr.	(for mister)

Esq.	(for esquire)
Mrs.	(for mistress)
M.	(for monsieur)
MM.	(for messieurs)
Mlle	(for mademoiselle)—no stop
Mme	(for madame)—no stop
Herr	(complete word)—no stop

13.

WORDS *v* FIGURES

Use words:

(*a*) for numbers one to nine inclusive;

(*b*) when the number is expressed in an indefinite manner, as: there were about three hundred people present;

(*c*) when a number commences a sentence;

(*d*) for ages, when expressed as ordinal numbers, e.g. he was in his twenty-third year;

(*e*) for the time of day, when 'o'clock' is used; figures should be employed with a.m. and p.m.;

(*f*) in cheques, estimates, and in legal and other documents where it is essential to ensure accuracy or to prevent the possibility of fraudulent alterations, it is usual to type both figures and words;

(*g*) when referring to street names, such as 'Seventeenth Avenue', but if a word precedes the number, it is optional whether it should be spelt out, as: 'West Fifteenth Street' or 'West 15th Street'.

Use figures:

(*a*) when the sign % is used;

(*b*) for dates, scores, weights, and numbers of houses in streets.

NOTE: Avoid mixing words and figures in the same sentence or phrase; type either 10,000 or ten thousand, but not 10 thousand.

14.

TYPEWRITING PAPER

For many years the most common sizes of paper used were:

Quarto 8″ by 10″ and Octavo 8″ by 5″

Now an international standard size of paper has been introduced the measurements of which are based on the metric system. The two sizes of paper most commonly used are:

A4 210 mm by 297 mm (8.27″ by 11.69″)
A5 210 mm by 148 mm (8.27″ by 5.84″)

A5 paper is exactly half the size of A4 paper. The former can be used with either the short or long dimension across the top.

Paper quantities: 24 sheets = 1 quire. 20 quires = 1 ream.
480 sheets = 1 ream.

15.

TYPING SUMS OF MONEY

The decimal currency is based on the pound sterling, but the pound is divided into a hundred new pence instead of twenty shillings. There were previously three units to measure money values: the pound, the shilling and the penny. The decimal pound, '£', (for 'libra') remains the abbreviation for the pound, and continues to be used before the number showing the amount. No full stop should be placed after the pound sign.

The penny was abbreviated to 'd.' (for 'denarius'), and the abbreviation followed the amount. It was suggested that 'np' should describe the 'new penny', but 'np' has the disadvantage of using two letters instead of one. If we had kept the 'd.' to describe the penny and used 'nd' for the new penny this could have led to confusion. For example, if we had '2nd' this could have been two new pennies or a date—the 2nd. So it was decided that the abbreviation should be 'p'. We have, therefore, 27p,

53p and so on. No full stop should be used after the 'p' unless it ends a sentence.

Apart from the £1 note there are three bronze copper coins:

$\frac{1}{2}$p (represents 1.2d. old currency)
1p (represents 2.4d. old currency)
2p (represents 4.8d. old currency)

three cupro-nickel coins:

5p (identical in value, size, weight and metal content to 1s. old currency)

10p (identical in value, size, weight and metal content to florin, old currency)

50p (10s.) which is a seven-sided coin.

When typing sums of money, only the pound and pence signs are used, so that sums of money appear as follows:

£25
£25.50
75p
52$\frac{1}{2}$p

NOTE:

(1) For amounts under a pound, e.g. 97p, use the form '97p' for general use and '£0.97' as a more formal expression.

(2) For mixed amounts, use the £ sign only, e.g. £29.27.

(3) Two digits should always be used in the pence column. Such a use will prevent confusion between, for example, 8p (£0.08) and 80p (£0.80).

(4) The new half penny is written as '$\frac{1}{2}$'. Thus 3$\frac{1}{2}$p will be written as £0.03$\frac{1}{2}$ or 3$\frac{1}{2}$p.

(5) The use of 'p' only for amounts above £1 is incorrect. Expressions such as '105p' (guinea) fail to recognize the pound.

16.

ABBREVIATIONS

These fall into two main groups:
   (*a*) abbreviations found in manuscripts and draft documents;
   (*b*) recognized abbreviations used in commerce.

   (i)   *Ampersand.* This would be used in typewriting only
         when it occurs in the name of a firm. It is used in the
         name of a firm even when this appears in the body of
         a letter.

   (ii) *e.g. viz. i.e.* When performing their true function as
         abbreviations, these are always preceded by a comma,
         but not followed by one.

   (iii) *Full stop.* Recognized abbreviations are indicated by
         the use of a full stop, but there are certain *symbols*
         which are not strictly abbreviations and these do not
         need the stop:

                        £
                        1st, 2nd, 3rd, etc.
                        per cent
                        Roman numerals

         It should also be noted that no points are required
         after Herts, Yorks, Salop, Hants, etc.

   (iv) *Re* is not a preposition or an abbreviation of 'reference'
         or 'referring', but part of the Latin phrase *in re*. It
         should not be used to precede a heading or instead of
         'with reference to'. If it is dictated the typist should
         not give it an abbreviation stop.

         The following are examples of abbreviations where
         two letters appear close together with no separating
         point:

                        pp.   pages
                        MS.   manuscript
                        MSS.   manuscripts

NOTE:

(1) As P.S. (post-script) represents the one word *postscriptum*, it seems unnecessary to separate the two letters by a point and some printers recommend the form PS.

(2) In printing, only a small space is allowed between the figure and the abbreviation in e.g. 421 litres. This practice cannot be followed in typing so a full space must be allowed as the same sign is used to represent small '1' as the figure '1'.

(3) It is not necessary to raise the point in percentages, e.g. 6.5%, or in sums of money, e.g. £6.50.

17.
CAPITALS

The modern tendency is to use lower case letters as far as possible. The following is a summary of instances in which initial capitals are essential:

(*a*) reference to the Deity and for all pronouns and synonyms relating thereto;

(*b*) festivals, days and months, and special events, as: Christmas, Michaelmas Day, the Reformation.

　　　NOTE:　The seasons, spring, summer, autumn and winter do not require initial capitals.

(*c*) compass points and names of roads and streets;

(*d*) titles of distinction and abbreviations, e.g. Sir, M.A., O.B.E.

(*e*) titles of books, plays, etc.;

(*f*) first letter of every line of poetry.

In ordinary literary matter the use of a capital letter will make an important difference to the meaning:

The *Band* of H.M. Scots Guards was surrounded by a *band* of admirers.

Sizes of typewriting paper

A4	210 mm × 297 mm
A5	210 mm × 148 mm

18.

METRICATION

An international system of weights and measures is being introduced and will be known as SI (*Système International d'Unités*).

Length is measured in metres
Mass is measured in kilograms
Volume is measured in cubic metres (but litres are also commonly used)
Power is measured in watts
Temperature is measured in degrees Celsius

Length
The unit is the metre, equal to 39.37 inches.
Long distances are measured in kilometres, approximately 5/8 mile.

Volume
The unit is the cubic metre but in common use is the litre, equal to $1\frac{3}{4}$ pints.

Weight/Mass
The unit is the kilogram: 500 grams, which equals half a kilogram, is just over a pound.

Power
The unit of power is the watt. We use both watts (for light bulbs, etc.) and kilowatts (for electric fires, etc.).

Temperature
The degree Celsius replaces the degree Centigrade. Zero degree Celsius is the freezing point and 100 degrees Celsius is the boiling point of water.

Rules for typing	*Reasons and examples*
Symbols are the same in the plural as they are in the singular.	1 m = one metre 10 m = ten metres
Never put a full stop after a symbol except at the end of a sentence.	They are symbols not abbreviations
Leave single space between figures and symbols.	1 kg

Avoid hyphenating a unit.	millimetres *not* milli- (next line) metres.
Use the correct case of type.	kg *not* Kg
To avoid confusion write 'litre' and 'tonne' in full	91 1 incorrectly written as 911 could be confused as nine hundred and eleven. The symbol for 'tonne' t is sometimes incorrectly used for (imperial) ton.

Note 'ton' and 'tonne' are pronounced the same, so to avoid confusion when speaking say 'metric tonne'.

Decimal Sign

The decimal sign is the point.

For weights and measures, the point is placed on the line in printed, handwritten and typed material, e.g. 1.505 m.

Thousands Marker

The space is to be used as the thousands marker.

Four figures or less may be blocked together, e.g.

1000 kg

1000 litres

Five figures or more are to be grouped in threes divided by single spaces, e.g.

10 000

1 000 000

BUT when tabulating numbers, all numbers should be grouped in threes to keep them in columns and to ensure clarity, e.g.

1 000

10 000

100 000

———

111 000

———

Note: the comma will be retained for indicating thousands in currency.

19.
METHOD OF ADDRESSING CORRESPONDENCE

The Post Office issues lists of post offices with their correct postal addresses and also directories of addresses for each area which has been allocated Postcodes.

Post Towns

These act as clearing points for a particular district and are key-points of the postal system, specially chosen for their accessibility.

The Post Town is a vital part of a postal address and should always be shown in BLOCK capitals.

Postcodes

A Postcode is a group of letters and figures which represents an address in abbreviated form, as an aid to automatic sorting. Postcodes have already been issued to many towns. Details of the appropriate Postcode have been sent to all addresses in each area, and all people living and working there are asked to use them as part of their normal address.

The Postcode should always appear in block capitals as the last item of information in any address.

Information about Postcodes can be obtained from Head Postmasters.

Example

The address should include in all cases:

1. Name of addressee
2. Number of the house
3. Name of the thoroughfare
4. Name of Post Town in BLOCK capitals
5. Postcode. This should always appear in BLOCK capitals as the last item of information in any address. (If the Postcode is not known the old Postal district should be used.)

The use of abbreviations for county names which are not postally acceptable is liable to cause confusion and lead to delay. The county name should be shown in full unless a shortened form for it appears in the following list of postally acceptable abbreviations:

Beds.	Bedfordshire	Lincs.	Lincolnshire
Berks.	Berkshire	Middx.	Middlesex
Bucks.	Buckinghamshire	Mon.	Monmouthshire
Cambs.	Cambridgeshire	Northants.	Northamptonshire
Carms.	Carmarthenshire	Northd.	Northumberland
Co. Derry	Co. Londonderry	Notts.	Nottinghamshire
Co. Durham	County Durham	Oxon.	Oxfordshire
Glam.	Glamorgan	Pembs.	Pembrokeshire
Glos.	Gloucestershire	Radnor.	Radnorshire
Hants.	Hampshire	Salop.	Shropshire
Herts.	Hertfordshire	Staffs.	Staffordshire
Lancs.	Lancashire	Wilts.	Wiltshire
Leics.	Leicestershire	Worcs.	Worcestershire